Eyewitness to War and Peace

Eamonn Mallie, a multi-award-winning journalist, is one of Ireland's most respected and well-known media personalities. Working as a reporter and political correspondent out of Belfast for over three decades, he covered every aspect of Northern Ireland's Troubles, interviewing figures including Nelson Mandela, Margaret Thatcher, Bill Clinton, John Major, Tony Blair, Mother Teresa, Bertie Ahern and Charles J. Haughey.

Eyewitness to War and Peace

Eamonn Mallie

MERRION
PRESS

First published in 2024 by
Merrion Press
10 George's Street
Newbridge
Co. Kildare
Ireland
www.merrionpress.ie

978 1 78537 506 4 (Paper)
978 1 78537 507 1 (Ebook)

A CIP catalogue record for this book is
available from the British Library.

Typeset in Calluna 12/17.5 pt

Cover design by riverdesignbooks.com

Front cover: © Pacemaker
Back cover courtesy of The White House

Merrion Press is a member of Publishing Ireland.

For Detta,
whom I affectionately call
'Lady Mallie'

Contents

Preface

I LOVED WORDS AS a child. Perhaps it was preordained that I would spend my life making a living from them. I always wanted to learn new words, firstly in English, then in Irish when I started learning it. Nothing changed when I moved to grammar school. I couldn't get enough new idioms in any language. I must have been a 'puke' asking teachers, 'How do you say such and such?' in Irish, French and Spanish. That was always the way I was – inquisitive. To this day I cannot let a word or a phrase pass me by without finding out the meaning of it. I hope when I die there is Google wherever I find myself. My grandchildren have already spotted this urge in me to continue learning. Teaching seven-year-old Eve a new word recently, she remarked, 'Papa you are weird, but I love you.'

I could be considered a bit eccentric, obsessed with literature, poetry, folklore, oral tradition and storytelling. I have instinctively gravitated towards older people over the years, many of them becoming my closest friends. I wanted to be in their company because they had worked out who they were. They had a life's experience and did not feel obliged to play at being something or somebody they weren't. I am now one of those older people, my friends dwindling in numbers. My wife, Detta, considers me elitist and regularly ticks me off when I am losing the run of myself about certain issues.

I always saw myself as an outsider. Politically I didn't really fit in, possibly due to my being born close to the South Armagh/Louth border, caught between two entities. In school we learned about Luther, Zwingli and Calvin. We didn't learn anything about the Easter Rising or the War of Independence in the Republic of Ireland, which happened the other side of the ditch from where I was reared. Writers and philosophers, such as Camus, Sartre and Unamuno among others, all contributed to my seeing the world through a certain lens. That said, one of my strengths, which has brought me a long way, is a readiness to try to understand why people behave the way they do.

My parents identified with the politics of Seamus Mallon and John Hume of the Social Democratic and Labour Party (SDLP). I was always an admirer of Hume's anti-violence and pro-European stances, but despite being of that disposition and hating political violence, I did not patronise those who pursued that path. I did not allow my opposition to the use of violence for political ends to be a reason to shun those who chose to take up arms to achieve their political goals. I wanted to understand why they felt the need to use violence.

I had an easy facility for connecting with anybody and everybody and undoubtedly this secured my relationship with DUP leader Ian Paisley. One might justifiably ask how a man from South Armagh (disgracefully labelled 'Bandit Country' by former Secretary of State Merlyn Rees) could hit it off with Paisley, who was perceived to be a rabble-rouser, a hater of all for which the Catholic Church stood and at the same time an arch critic of everything about the Republic of Ireland. All I can say is that from the first moment of meeting Paisley outside his Cypress Avenue home in East Belfast, right up until the end of his life, I felt at home in his company. He fascinated me and for that reason I pushed for him to allow me to record his life story. People are people and I always argue, 'get to know each other and anything is possible'. I haven't ever had a problem talking to a member of the Irish Republican Army (IRA), Ulster Defence Association (UDA) or Ulster Volunteer Force (UVF), and I have engaged with hundreds of them over the years.

So why did I decide to write an account of my life as a journalist? It was Detta who suggested it and I wasn't averse to the idea. As an historian constantly burgling the research and scholarship of others, I felt it would be useful to reflect in print on both the good and bad times I saw through working at the coalface in Northern Ireland for nearly half a century. Furthermore, I feel much freer now, with the passing of the years, to be more forthright in unwrapping what, of necessity, could not be publicly aired at the height of the Troubles. It has been one hell of a trip discovering through further research for this book what was actually taking place well away from my gaze down the years.

On 3 March 1977 I was sitting in the Downtown Radio newsroom when word reached us that the last prime minister of Northern Ireland, Brian Faulkner, was dead. He had fallen from his horse while out hunting. In those days we didn't have Google or Wikipedia. I overheard my duty editor, Paddy O'Flaherty, calling a rival Belfast newsroom and saying to one of the reporters, 'Would you have a few lines of background on Brian Faulkner?' When Paddy came off the phone I said to him, 'Is it not embarrassing having to phone another news desk to get information about a breaking story? Have we no archives of our own?' 'There are times when you have to go down a rat hole for a story,' Paddy told me.

Over the next forty years and more I went down that rat hole in pursuit of the story, and more often than not I poked in a hole with no rat in it, but Paddy's lesson was well learned. It was going to the ends of the earth for the story that defined me professionally throughout my years working in the media. It was a ruthless pursuit of the story and the truth that underscored my drive to hold people to account for their actions, whether in government, in illegal organisations, in Churches or in other areas of public life. It was through doing exactly this that I established my reputation for 'breaking' stories, much to the displeasure of government and the establishment on many occasions.

Journalists love nothing better than a scoop and I've had my fair share over the years. Revelation has always been grist to my mill as a journalist. Turning over the pages of this book I hope, again and again, your response will be, 'I didn't know that.'

Chapter One

A Border Child

I WAS A POST-WAR baby boomer, born on 16 July 1950. I have always seen myself as a 'border child', entering the world in South Armagh, a stone's throw from County Louth in the Republic of Ireland. Like many families before ours, and after, we felt economically abandoned by the Unionist-dominated government at Stormont and the Irish government in Dublin. There was no fancy cradle awaiting me on arrival in this world. My father often reminded me that I started out life in a drawer.

My mother, Eileen McKeever, was born and reared in the predominantly nationalist townland of Dorsey, close to Cullyhanna in South Armagh. She met my father, Michael Mallie, in 1947, the year of the big snow, close to her home at a dance in Wylie's loft. Mum was still a teenager when she and Dad married – my older brother Michael was born the following year. My mother's teacher, Mrs Nellie Muckian, had spotted her academic prowess and furnished her with the appropriate application forms to take a forthcoming examination, confident that she would be successful. However, she soon became a teenage mum with childcaring responsibilities, and that put an end to the prospect of any further education. She had six children by the time she was thirty. Mum often told us how she burned those forms, but her lost opportunity lived with her, and she was determined that her children should get every chance in life.

My father, locally called Mickey, was born and reared on a farm in Cargan, a townland about eight miles from where my mum was born but further south, looking towards Dundalk. Dad's home was a big, elegant, two-storey, slate-roofed house standing high upon a hill, with a commanding view over the valley. Granny Mallie was a keen gardener, who was very proud of her flowers and vegetables. Granda Mallie was born posthumously – his father, also called Michael, had gone to England in search of work and perished in a steel works in a sea of moulten metal. Granda was a pet. He was easy-going, and I loved it when he played the concertina. He enjoyed a song as well. He really liked Mum and she loved him.

Daddy worked on the land for the first twenty-six years of his life. On marrying my mum, he ceased to work the home farm. His brother, Peter, who – like my aunt Mary – had been sent to grammar school, came home and took over. Daddy didn't really talk to us about his ceasing to farm the homeplace, but he often cautioned us, 'Don't ever squabble over land or money.'

My parents' first home was at Carrive crossroads, about two miles away from where Dad was reared. In stark contrast to his family home, we had no electricity, no running water and my parents often spoke of having to be vigilant, fearing the arrival of a rat in this dilapidated, rented house. No longer working on the home farm meant that my father was forced to find any job he could, so from time to time he had to leave Mum – firstly with one child, then with two and so on – to go in search of

6

work in England or Belfast. I remember him leaving home one day and having to borrow the price of his boat fare to England from Mickey Garvey, a local businessman. Such was the poverty of a border area like South Armagh in the fifties and early sixties that most local men 'took the boat' at one time or another.

My brother Michael was the eldest of the family; I was born next. Goretti was after me, followed by Anthony, Peadar and then Carmel, the baby. My mother told me there was a dispute over what name to give me right up until the last minute. My Granny Mallie wanted me to be called Edward, after her brother, but Mum certainly didn't want that – she didn't want me to be nicknamed Ned or something worse in the schoolyard. As I was being carried out the door to be christened, Mum shouted to my godparents, 'Call him Eamonn after Eamonn Mallie in Newtownhamilton.' That family was not directly related to us – my mum just liked the way the names ran together.

She used to joke that she had three 'drummers' – a reference to the Orangemen's marching season in Northern Ireland. Michael was born on the fifteenth of July, I was born on the sixteenth and Goretti on the twenty-fifth. Looking back, I suspect the coincidence of three of us having our birthdays in July was linked to the time of year my father was usually back home from England, where he spent many years working. For my mum, our being Catholic and born in the marching season in Northern Ireland had a certain irony. In Dorsey, where she had grown up, there had been a knot of Protestant homes. Those neighbours left a lasting imprint on Mum's life and on our lives as children too. Down through the years she spoke warmly about the Wylies, the Henrys, the Palmers and other Protestant children she had known. She told us many times about her Protestant childhood friends joining her and her family in reciting the Rosary in her home. She always said that she wanted to be buried 'with the Protestants' in Creggan graveyard, so we buried her there, and Dad sleeps beside her.

After living at Carrive for a couple of years, we moved to O'Neill Park in Cregganduff, between Silverbridge and Crossmaglen. During our time there, I was wracked with chest trouble and as a result I didn't start school until I was over six years old, and I was a year behind my contemporaries right through to university. Eventually my father and mother settled on a smallholding in Legmoylin, close to Silverbridge, which my father's parents bought for them. We had seven acres of land (scarcely enough to rear a snipe) with a large two-storey whitewashed house. Legmoylin was my Shangri-La. The house was located at the bottom of a quarter-mile-long lane on the side of a valley, looking onto my grandparents' home on the other side of the Cully Water River. There was no running water in our house – except down the walls – and no electricity. We were totally dependent on a Tilley lamp for our lighting. The old Tilley lamp was paraffin fuelled, with a mantle which was lit with a match. That Tilley lamp would make an incalculable contribution to my education, not just because it afforded me light but because it contributed so much to my enlightenment.

With six children and only two bedrooms, sleeping arrangements were tight. In the dead of winter, it wasn't uncommon for Mum to throw every overcoat in the house over us at night to give us a bit of extra heat. As the wind howled in under the bottom of the front door, my father would remark, 'You could glean corn with that draught', tucking a rolled-up meal bag into the gap. Our bedroom was next to our parents' room and when

Dad was away working somewhere, many a night I found myself awake listening to Mum snoring. All of a sudden there would be silence. Fearing she had died, I used to slip into her bedroom to give her a gentle nudge to make sure she was still breathing.

Though we hadn't much upon which to come and go, we were happy. Mum had a great saying: 'We may not be rich, but we can wash clean.' That described our modus vivendi. We got on with life, and my mother kept an immaculate house. She was obsessive about hygiene. It was customary around home to send the Christmas turkey to McNamee's bakery in Crossmaglen to be cooked in their ovens. Mum always feared that she might not get her own turkey home; that there might be a mix-up. She came up with an ingenious solution – she placed a spoon beneath one of the wings of the turkey and sewed it into place. When she got the cooked turkey back, she checked for the spoon. When Dad was not at home, the soundtrack to which Mum lived in the evenings was Radio Luxembourg. Local girls Kitty, Billie and Rosaleen McShane used to come to our house three or four nights a week for a sing-song. They were all daft on music. Of course, in those days you had Elvis emerging as a superstar, and then there was Brenda Lee, Bill Haley and Lonnie Donegan and his famous washboard.

As a child, I had two big interests in life: fishing and hunting. I loved chasing pheasants, rabbits and hares across the countryside with my favourite dog, Rex, the king of the land. My mother always knew where to find me – if I wasn't away with the dog, I was on the riverbank. I used to fish day and night. In my early childhood days, I was an expert at cupping my hands around a stone in the river and trapping a trout beneath. Only once do I recall sinning against nature in the Cully Water river

– Michael and I limed a pool, having been set a bad example by older boys. The shame of being party to that action lingers – the sight of those upturned bellies floating on the water's surface will always be my My Lai massacre. Apart from my fishing and hunting there were chores, but we didn't see them as such. We regularly had to haul home a zinc bathtub full of fresh water from a spring well about fifteen minutes away. Necessity was the mother of invention: to ease our burden, Michael and I threaded a thick hazel rod through the two eyes of the handles of the tub, making it easier to carry.

One of the highlights of our year was the arrival of the threshing mill in our haggard. It was our equivalent to one of the great fiestas that I saw in Spain as a student. Just as the ritual of the threshing of the corn played a part in our lives once a year, so too did the arrival of those we called 'our gypsies' – the Joyces. We called them 'our gypsies' deliberately and I was fascinated by them. Over the years, we got to know them personally as they came to our home to mend buckets, cans and saucepans, an invaluable service to us in an underdeveloped community. As Seamus Heaney writes in his poem 'Tall Dames': 'Every time they landed in the district an extra-ness in the air, as if a gate had been left open in the usual life, as if something might get in or get out.'

Like thousands of other impoverished mothers on the island of Ireland, my mother saw education as the passport to a better way of life for her children. Our neighbours were taken aback when she purchased the *Oxford Dictionary and Encyclopaedia* at a cost of twenty-one guineas to be paid over twenty-one months. That was a lot of money back in those days. She often told us, 'Read! I don't care what you read, whether it's the *Beano* or the *Dandy*, as long as you read.' Funnily enough, I didn't read comics. I had no interest in them, with the result that my brothers often accuse me of having a very poor sense of humour. I tend to be more serious in terms of the books I choose, and I suppose it was that lust for learnedness that pushed me on, eventually to university.

I was unfortunate in both my primary schools. I didn't enjoy life as a child in the local school at Silverbridge, mainly because I didn't connect with my teachers. My parents, unhappy with our education, sent us instead to the Christian Brothers' primary school in Newry. My experience was little better there. I arrived at the school ten months before the eleven-plus and found myself at the back of the class. I felt humiliated, but it was a great lesson – I would rise up again. I didn't pass the eleven-plus and ended up at St Joseph's secondary school in Newry. It was there that a young teacher called Miss McCarthy spotted my aptitude for languages. Injudiciously, she paraded me in front of another class that she was teaching to demonstrate my ability to speak French. I didn't see it as being harmful back then, but on reflection I wonder how the other children must have felt. It was the wrong thing to do, however well-intentioned Miss McCarthy was.

I got what was known as 'the Review' – a second-chance eleven-plus – after one and a half years at St Joseph's. With a scholarship, I went to the Abbey Grammar and, in fairness to the Christian Brothers, I had an enjoyable time there, study-ing under some of the most brilliant educationalists I have ever met – exceptional teachers like Hugh Murphy, who taught me Latin and Irish; Brendan Cassidy; Patsy Rice; Tommy Keane, who taught me French; and Jack Cushnahan, who taught me Spanish. I hold nothing against the Christian Brothers' education, apart from one thing: they didn't teach me Greek. I enjoyed Latin, and in many ways I regret that I didn't do it for A level. One day, Brother McCrohan sneeringly asked me, 'Where are you going, Mallie, if you get your exams?' 'To Trinity College,' I replied. 'Oh, that den of iniquity,' he answered. I fired back, 'They are all dens of iniquity.'

A shortage of money was not unusual in our home. One morning, I came down the stairs and told Mum I wasn't going to school. 'I can't go into school without three pounds for the capital fee [a charge levied on every pupil used for the school's building fund]. There are only two of us left in the class at the end of two weeks who haven't paid it.' Mum broke down and cried. She didn't have the money to give to me and the school was asking me for it every day.

My brother Michael, who was strong at maths, ended up going to Bessbrook Tech, where he enjoyed life in a mixed Catholic/Protestant environment, played a lot of football and felt very much at home. It was there he met his-wife-to-be, Alice Boyle, and thank God they have lived happily ever after, rearing their family and now babysitting their grandchildren on a regular basis. One big advantage flowing from Michael's time in Bessbrook Tech was that he brought home to our tea table the Protestant version of Grace before meals, and as a family we then regularly used the two versions, the Protestant and the Catholic.

Goretti and Carmel both went to the Poor Clares' convent in Newry, where they were taught by nuns and lay teachers. Goretti was the life and soul of the party when we were teenagers – how she loved to dance and have the craic. Anthony, who came after Goretti, has inherited many of our mother's gifts – primarily, her photographic memory. I refer to him as the oracle. When I am trying to recall a saying, a phrase or some fact about life during our childhood, I call Anthony and invariably he knows the answer. Peadar, who himself claims to have the best memory in our family, cut short his schooling. He was a capable footballer who became a joiner and today has an endless stream of extraordinary sayings and witticisms, many of which I borrow and retail. He could entertain a nation and is rarely found wanting for a killer one-liner. Carmel will always be the baby of the family in my eyes. She was a beautiful, sweet child.

I was the only wanderer in the family – my five siblings thankfully found gainful employment in the immediate area where we grew up, on each side of the border. One of the proudest moments in my year is sitting down as a family, and extended family, in the Canal Court Hotel, Newry, for our annual dinner in the run-up to Christmas. I see this 'togetherness' as one of the great gifts our parents left to us. I trust the in-laws – Alice, Eileen, Brendan, Tony and Detta – are as relaxed with us as we are breaking bread with them. Sadly, we lost Peadar's wife, Marian, in August 2021. John McParland, the hotelier who stands us a drink every year after our dinner, gets away lightly, with only a few at the table drinking alcohol.

Church was important to us as a family, and each Sunday we walked close on three miles to Glassdrummond Chapel. During the Mission (a week dedicated to prayer every three years) we walked there even more frequently. When we reached the top of Fearon's Brae, we could spot the church away in the distance, across the countryside. Michael used to say, 'Wouldn't it be great to jump into a helicopter and land at the chapel immediately?' Today, my little grandson Rory talks about teleporting. When he first mentioned this to me, I had to ask him what he meant. What none of us as children of the fifties and sixties could have foreseen was that in future decades, Michael's children would grow up with the skies in South Armagh full of British Army helicopters.

As an emerging teenager, I was decidedly prayerful, moving halfway up the church to be closer to God while many of my contemporaries from around home took up positions during Mass in the church porch, smoking, joking and laughing. One Sunday, the excitable Father McFadden shouted down from the pulpit about 'farmyard sex'. 'All you want to do is dance, date and vegetate,' he said.

One of the great influences in my life was my aunt Mary, my father's sister. She worked in the Imperial Civil Service in London, returned to the Civil Service at Stormont and ended up a tax officer in Newry. She was almost forty when she married a laicised Christian Brother, Brendan Hanna. There was always a distance between my mum and my grandmother, my father's mother, but as far back as I can remember my aunt Mary took my mum under her wing, taking care of her. She loved Mum like the sister she didn't have. She and Brendan came to our house every Sunday evening to have tea with us. They were both obsessed with education. Invariably, they arrived armed with a copy of the latest *Reader's Digest*. We used to get threepence or sixpence for each word that we knew from the *Digest* dictionary – I can assure you they hadn't to shell out much money in our earlier years. It was always fun and so many of those words that I learned back then travelled with me all down through the years: words like pugnacious, ostentatious, sagacious, peripatetic and so on. My aunt and her husband enriched our lives. Aunt Mary bought my dad's winter clothing, quite often bought our school uniforms and would regularly buy something for Mum. We were blessed to have her; sadly she died in 2021, just short of her 100th birthday.

Families in the countryside in our part of the world can be dotted quite a distance apart from each and yet we were interdependent. Peter Grant pulled out in his van many a day and went to Carraher's at Silverbridge or to Lavelle's shop at the border and returned with a bag of coal for us, having realised the fire in our stove wasn't lit. There were other great people who helped us and who were generous to us as children. There was the McAvoy family – Mary, Arthur and their sons Jim and Patsy – lifelong friends of my parents and friends of ours to this day. As a student I used to travel in McAvoys' meat lorries to spend some time in France or Belgium, or wherever I was going. McAvoys' drivers brought a little bit of France back to the locals in the pub at home. It was not uncommon for two of the guys who were back and forward to France to kiss each other on both cheeks when they met in the local bar – to the consternation of the locals.

The McAvoys were the first people in our townland to have a television, and I recall clearly the November night in 1963 that Mum, Michael and I went céilíing there, only to learn that President John F. Kennedy had been shot dead in Dallas. That was the biggest news story of my lifetime at that point. It was extraordinary for us as young people. The news was delivered by Charles Mitchell on RTÉ. Little did Mitchell know that I dreamed of one day doing his job. When I finally got my chance, I proved to be the worst newsreader ever heard on radio, but fortunately I had other arrows in my quiver. We also used to go to the McAvoys to watch *Bonanza* and *The Virginian*. We loved those shows.

My parents used to regularly visit the home of our other great neighbours – the Fearons. Katie Fearon, who was married to Felie Boyle, was the cornerstone of that house. One of my fondest recollections of dropping into that home was Katie making orange sandwiches for us coated in sugar. To us as children, Katie ran a two-star Michelin kitchen.

I can't remember Michael without an O'Neill's All-Ireland football in his hand when we were growing up. I didn't have the same dedication to the sport that he and Anthony had, but the first heroes in my life were members of our local football team. I was only nine years old when Silverbridge beat Ballyhegan in the Armagh Junior Football Championship final in 1959. I grow nostalgic when I think of that wonderful afternoon. I can still see my father shouldering high some of our heroes after their victory. Also from the sport came the only saint from my childhood – Peter Keeley, our team manager. He was the first to give me a 'run-out' in a 'Bridge jersey in a game of football. As he nervously moved up and down the sideline and even halfway onto the pitch during matches, he chewed an acre of grass, snatching at wisps of it, as a rake of *gasúns* (boys) begged him to put them on. Even if we were winning a crucial game by a mere point, Keeley was inclined to take off the best player on the field and replace him with a guy with two left feet. Somebody like myself. His defence: 'Sheo, the *gasún* needs a run-out.' He represented humanity and kindness in his concern for children of all abilities.

Years later, in 2002, Armagh won the All-Ireland, the most prestigious and coveted achievement in Gaelic games, for the first time. Unless one is born into a Gaelic Athletic Association (GAA) family, it is hard to understand what that means to any county and the soul of its people. Michael, who was an Armagh County Minor steeped in the GAA, was given the Sam Maguire trophy – the cup awarded to the winning team – for a night by one of Armagh's famous sons, Steven McDonnell. The Sam Maguire trophy is bigger to GAA fans than an Olympic medal. I watched my father crying that day when Michael handed him that Holy Grail of Gaelic football. The Sam Maguire had eluded my father in his playing days, as it had thousands of other young footballers. When Michael brought 'Sam' in to his old neighbours, the McCoys, to show it to them, Pete also started to cry, just as my dad had. His wife, Josie, told Michael, 'Hold on until I take out my curlers. I can't get my photograph taken with the Sam Maguire cup, and my curlers in.'

To salute the success of the Armagh team, the Northern Ireland Assembly members invited them to Stormont for a reception. Among those present in Parliament Buildings that evening were Tyrone Sinn Féin Member of the Legislative Assembly (MLA) Michelle Gildernew with her husband, Jimmy, and baby son, Emmet. Michelle and her husband had cheekily dressed baby Emmet in Tyrone colours that night (Tyrone people don't like Armagh people because of football rivalry and vice versa). Spotting a photo opportunity, Gerry Adams popped little Emmet into the cup. Michelle Gildernew feigning embarrassment about a Tyrone baby in Armagh's Sam Maguire didn't fool me. The same woman is no wilting violet.

***

My interest in the Irish language was sparked by a few words I had heard spoken by my aunt Biddy's brother-in-law, P.J. Campbell, whose mother was a native Donegal Gaelic speaker. I don't know how fluent he was in Irish, but he knew enough to trigger my curiosity. No one in my immediate family spoke the language – I simply liked what I heard from old P.J. Realising my interest, my mum and dad arranged for me to go to a summer school in Omeath when I was seven or eight. I went there for several weeks and I loved it. There was a very special occasion when the future Cardinal Tomás Ó Fiaich, then a very young priest, arrived with the last Gaelic speaker from the entire Cooley Peninsula in County Louth. Her name was Nelly Ó hAnluain. It was fascinating to hear somebody who was born almost a century earlier speaking Irish, essentially now a dead language in that corner of Ulster.

After Omeath, it was inevitable that I would start going to Donegal, to the Gaeltacht. From the age of thirteen, I went there for three weeks or a month each summer – sometimes to Ros Goill, sometimes to Teelin, sometimes to Ranafast and to Gweedore as well. I don't remember an unhappy moment during those summers learning Irish in Donegal. In fact, we nearly all fell in love for the first time in those days. It was there we experienced our first kiss and how we loved the céilí dances, and particularly walking the girls home at the end of the evening. We were all crazy about the pop music of the time, the Beatles and the Rolling Stones. One year, in the house in which we were staying, Teach Hudaí Bhig in Middledore, somebody, for a prank, told one of my classmates that Paul McCartney had died. The young man cried like a baby.

One of the people who accompanied me to Donegal was my

very best school friend, Jim McCooey, whom I had got to know at the start of my first year in Abbey Grammar. Jim, who came from Newtownhamilton, was born into a family business – his parents owned a shop at Cloughreagh, close to Bessbrook. The two of us, along with Maurice Connolly, were inseparable when we were at school. We had one hobby in common – we were fanatical about fishing. We used to go fishing every Saturday all over Armagh and Monaghan. One morning, we took a lift with my dad and a friend while it was still dark to Tullynawood Lake near Darkley – a lake famous for its rainbow trout. It was so early that we had to use stones to break the ice to start fishing. It was not uncommon for Jim and me to come home from the lake, possibly from Lough Muckno in Monaghan or possibly from somewhere in Armagh, as the carnival – the annual showband extravaganza – was ending at Ford's Cross near Silverbridge, such was our dedication and commitment to fishing.

As Jim and I grew older, he was able, coming from a well-off family, to buy a car. In those days I was penniless, but I didn't want for anything as long as Jim was around. I travelled to dances with him; he paid for my Coca-Cola and for my entrance to the dance. He was an extraordinary man throughout my whole life. My parents, my brothers and sisters all loved him. He was a giver. He married Betty, but sadly lost her when his children were still quite young. He battled on and reared his family, and I would regularly drop into the shop when visiting my parents and we would pick up on the conversation which we had left off when we were eleven or twelve years of age. The bond was rock solid right to the very end.

Some years ago, I learned that Jim had been hit with cancer. I spent the next eighteen months visiting him in hospital, or simply meeting him when he came out of the hospital in Belfast after a check-up. It was like being back in my early years in grammar school with him. We revisited much of the turf and the territory we both enjoyed so much, whether on the bank of the lake, on the riverbank or out hunting rabbits or duck, pheasant or whatever. Jim died on 15 April 2020. Sadly, because of Covid, I couldn't go to the hospice to see him. I couldn't even go to his funeral. Near the end, Jim's daughter Eimear called me to let me know her dad was deteriorating. I said, 'Eimear, tell your dad I love him.' It was the first time in my life I had told a grown man that I loved him. I genuinely did love Jim. He was one of the best friends I ever had, but cancer took him away. I hope one day I will be reunited with him.

In his poem 'A Call', Seamus Heaney writes of a conversation on the phone with his mother when he tells her he would like a word with his father. Eventually his father is on the other end of the line and Heaney writes, 'Next thing he spoke and I nearly said I loved him.' That poem gave me the courage to tell Jim that I loved him. I am hurting now that I didn't ever say to my dad, 'I love you.'

***

My siblings and I are all older today than Mum was when she died from heart trouble on her fifty-ninth birthday in 1991. We have all benefitted from medical advances. From the day that Mum died, I always thought that Dad was dying. In fact, he lived for almost twelve more years, but it seemed to me that he was always waiting to see her again. Those years he was spared were so rewarding for me as a son, and I discovered a lot about my father as he and I grew older. He had been away from home quite a lot when we were growing up and I had gone to the Gaeltacht every summer from the start of my teens, so I probably didn't engage with him as much as I might have during my childhood. Dad was a man who was very rich in idiom. He had wonderful sayings and he had a wealth of anecdotes and stories that he had picked up from the old people. Perhaps having left home and having gone a-wandering, I appreciated these stories more. The older I get, the more I travel back home in my head.

There are times I think I am my father. When he finished his cup of tea, usually sitting in his favourite chair, he would toss his cup up in the air with one hand and flick it into his other hand. I sometimes find myself unconsciously doing exactly the same thing. I also inherited another of my dad's practices. He always came to our bedrooms when he was going to bed to say goodnight to us, even if we were fast asleep. He would give us a kiss and lay his hand upon our heads. It was something of a ritual. When my children came along, I carried on the tradition. Those are the little things in life that simply live with you. They don't leave you no matter how old you are. These days, my father's sayings suddenly come flooding into my head and I get lost enjoying and celebrating those moments.

When Mum was alive, Dad simply didn't answer the phone. She answered the phone. That said, he was always in the background saying, 'tell him this, tell him that, ask him this, ask him that'. When Mum died, it all changed. No matter where I was in the world, I called Dad every morning and discovered a very intelligent man, a much more learned man than I realised, and a man with a wonderful wit, who was great fun. I called him several times one morning but there was no answer. Eventually

I got him and asked, 'Where have you been all morning?' 'Eamonn,' he said, 'do you not realise there are ambassadors from all over the world calling me every morning to consult me on very important affairs. You are not the only one who rings me in the morning. Yours is not the only call.'

I also found out that Dad had a very keen, politically aware brain. I was involved in politics day and night – talking to politicians, interviewing politicians, listening to politicians – but some of the observations and pearls of wisdom that dropped from his lips surprised me. One morning, around the time of the Good Friday Agreement referendum, he said to me, 'You know, Eamonn, do you see that oul' bugger Trimble? There's a side to that man. I think he'll do business.' He had read the Ulster Unionist Party (UUP) leader correctly – in the wake of the 1998 Good Friday Agreement, David Trimble chose to bring his team into government with republicans, breaking the unionist mould.

My father was a man of great taste. His green and brown suits always toned with his chestnut-brown eyes. He took great pride in being properly groomed and, like myself, wore his hair slightly longer, out of sync with his contemporaries as he grew older. In fact, I inherited a kink in my hair which had originally found a home in his. There was nothing he liked more than to waltz around the floor with my mum, in step with The Kilfenora Céilí Band.

When Dad died suddenly in 2003, sitting in front of the television, Michael, Peadar and Anthony carried him upstairs to his bedroom and laid him out there in readiness for his wake. I am forever indebted to them. I consider what they did as having a certain biblical, spiritual dimension to it – carrying their own father in death as he had done for them a thousand times and more in life when they were children. While Dad was fortunate in having my brothers living nearby after Mum died, Goretti and Carmel also rendered an extraordinary service to him, caring for him as he grew older.

I still see my father and mother dancing in my mind's eye. I hoped I would have inherited their talent, but some years back, during one of our family weddings, one of my sisters brought me back down to earth with a bang, declaring, 'Eamonn, we didn't realise just how bad a dancer you are.' I knew then I was back home.

Chapter Two

Meeting My Galway Girl

IN THE SUMMER OF 1970, after I had completed my A levels, I left home and started to travel more widely. London was my first port of call. I lived with three friends from home – Maurice Connolly, Tom Hughes and Joe McNally – in a dump of a house in Shepherd's Bush and laboured on a building site in Harefield. I hated every minute of it and resented being called Mick, Paddy or Mate. I determined that summer that I would not spend my life as a labourer with the pub as the big prize at the weekend.

As soon as I finished on the building site, I flew to San Sebastián in the Basque Country, where I taught English in an academy. I lived with Patsy Rice, one of my former teachers from the Abbey in Newry, who was lecturing in a Jesuit College near the city. Patsy was a fine linguist, and his children's first words were *aitona eta amona* (grandfather and grandmother) in Basque.

It is extraordinary what children and teenagers of today take for granted in terms of communication. My mum received just one short letter from me that first summer I spent in Spain. Franco was in power and *la minifalda* (the miniskirt) had not yet arrived. The miniskirt worn by an English girl on the bus in which I was travelling one day almost caused the driver to crash as he craned his neck trying to get a good look at her. To him, her *minifalda* was clearly one of the great Wonders of the World.

The Abbey Grammar was not a natural feeder for Trinity College Dublin (TCD), but romance and reading influenced my decision to study there. I was very much into the whole philosophy of existentialism at the time, reading writers like Samuel Beckett and Conor Cruise O'Brien, as well as works by thinkers, philosophers and poets who had been students there. I had also come across a group of Donegal Protestants in the Gaeltacht who were at Trinity and were wonderful exponents of all manifestations of Irish culture. Undoubtedly, my parents were particularly proud that I was going to university – the first member of my family to do so. There was a bigger factor at play, however. I was going through a rebellious period and there was a ban on Catholics going to TCD, which only made me want to go more. As it turned out, the ban was lifted in 1970, just as I arrived. By now I was well into my teenage years, obsessed with existentialism and alternative philosophies to my inherited Catholicism. Certainly, the contemptible response of Brother McCrohan about TCD when I told him I hoped to go there only served to make me more determined to defy the Catholic Church.

Trinity was quaint in so many ways in those days. When I occasionally attended Commons, the evening meal, in the dining hall, the doors were banged shut before a scholar stood up and intoned Grace in Latin: '*Oculi omnium in te sperant, Domine ...*' ('The eyes of all await upon thee, Lord ...'). The tradition had an air of pomposity about it, but it dated back centuries. It was also an experience very different to rhyming off the Rosary on our knees at home in Legmoylin. I loved my

Trinity College days. I even loved every cobblestone in Front Square – unlike my future wife, Detta, who hated them, finding them so hard to negotiate in her fashionable shoes and boots.

Those who didn't know me then might find it hard to believe that during my student years I worked as a DJ in a nightclub at the back of Trinity called The Squirrel's Nest. It was owned by Harold Armstrong of Castlederg, County Tyrone, whose sister Lorna was in college with me. I loved spinning those discs into the early hours of the morning. Such was the cosmopolitan mix at Trinity that I was able to mingle with people from all over the world, as well as people from closer to home. My Trinity days were enriched by a wonderful international tapestry of cultures.

The excitement of leaving home in Northern Ireland in September 1970 and heading off to college in Dublin eclipsed my interest in what was actually happening on the ground north of the border, as well as the continuing conflict in Vietnam. I was enjoying my freedom, making my own decisions and answerable to nobody as a student meeting new people. Then, in August 1971, two days before internment was introduced, Harry Thornton, a local man from home who was well known to my father, was shot dead by a soldier on the Springfield Road in West Belfast. The army opened fire on Thornton and the passenger in his vehicle, Arthur Murphy, claiming they thought a gun had been fired but, in reality, the van had backfired. Years later, coroner Brian Sherrard told the Thornton family, 'The shooting of Mr Thornton was neither a necessary, nor a reasonable, nor a proportionate, response to the situation. Mr Thornton was unarmed and no weapon was found during a search of a van, despite claims by Soldier C that he had seen a gun protruding from the van.' In 2012, the government wrote a letter of apology to Thornton's widow, Mary, confirming that her husband had been an 'innocent man'.

I recall the mood changed completely in the countryside after the killing of Harry Thornton. The first two British soldiers killed in an IRA attack in South Armagh were James Lee and Terence Graham, who died in a land mine explosion on the Carran Road outside Crossmaglen in 1972. Meanwhile, I was getting on with my college life, heading off to Spain and other places during the summers.

Then, on 17 May 1974, the violence of Northern Ireland arrived on my doorstep in Dublin. That was the day when three no-warning bombs exploded in Dublin, and a fourth went off in Monaghan about an hour and a half later. One of the Dublin bombs blew up at the intersection of Nassau Street and South Leinster Street, near the railings of Trinity College. I can still see the limb in a boot that I saw in the aftermath of that explosion. The bombs had been planted by loyalists, who had pledged to topple the power-sharing executive at Stormont that had been established as a result of the 1973 Sunningdale Agreement. That agreement had envisaged a cross-border Council of Ireland, which was like a red rag to a bull for hard-line unionists. During the two-week Ulster Workers' Council strike that ran from 15 to 28 May 1974 to demonstrate the unionists' opposition to Sunningdale, loyalists killed thirty-nine civilians, of whom thirty-three died in Dublin and Monaghan. Little did I know back then that I would go on to spend the next twenty years at the coalface in Northern Ireland, covering bombings, shootings and killings.

***

While in Trinity, I played Gaelic football. I deluded myself for years that I had played Sigerson Cup football, but the annals of the competition appear to be incomplete for the years I was there! I have now discovered that Trinity did not win one game in the Sigerson Cup competition during my time, let alone the cup itself. Perhaps if Tom Kennedy and Pat Doherty, who managed the Sigerson teams from 1971 to 1974, had been a little more perspicacious and let me take the field, who knows what would have happened. Trophies in the cabinet?

Even though I didn't make the Sigerson Cup team, I did have a trophy to show for my Gaelic football prowess, having played on a successful seven-a-side team in those years. One of those who played with me was Dick Spring, future tánaiste and Labour Party leader. Dick played Gaelic football and hurling for Kerry during the 1970s, and rugby for Trinity and Ireland, going on to win three caps for Ireland during the 1979 Five Nations Championship. If you could have heard the two of us recently, discussing our seven-a-side win, you would have thought we were World Cup winners.

The little things in life matter more to us as we grow older. In the course of our conversation, Dick told me that his small cup from that day had gone missing twenty years ago when his family moved house. He wondered whether I might be able to forward him a photograph of mine. No such luck – our attic at home was flooded when my parents died and everything, including my trophy, was dumped. Isn't that a coincidence? I loved that trophy – the only one I ever won.

The three Deeny brothers – Arthur, Godfrey and Donnell – filled a large space in TCD and everybody knew them. Donnell would go on to become a Court of Appeal judge in Northern

Ireland. In those Trinity years, he cut quite a dash crossing Front Square as auditor of the College Historical Society, in his gown, white tie and white tails, normally with the charming Sheila, his then girlfriend, on his arm. Donnell married Sheila, then, later, he married the stylish and effervescent Alison. I didn't really know Deeny well back then, but I had decided I didn't like him – he came across as somewhat aloof – but life is a great teacher. When I came to work in Belfast, I got to know him bit by bit and I discovered a gentleman and, above all, a man of principle.

When I was in Trinity, my good friend Joe Revington, president of the Students' Representative Council (later the Students' Union), used to say regularly in his beautiful Kerry lilt, 'Jaysus, Mallie, if it is the last thing we do before we leave here, we will get you drunk.' I didn't ever touch alcohol – drink was not part of our upbringing. Joe took enough for the two of us while we were at TCD but, thank God, he left all that behind him. Dick Spring, as Labour Party leader and tánaiste, was loyal to Joe after college. He took him under his wing and Joe didn't look back, having taken up law, working on the Munster Circuit as a Senior Counsel. From the first day of my knowing Joe, an elegant Derry woman, Finola O'Donnell, was always with him and she remained so until his death in 2021. We always knew it was getting close to *leaba* (bed) time when Joe stepped up onto a chair in the students' Buttery Bar and broke into 'The Rose of Tralee'. That was the Trinity Rosary!

Broadly speaking, individuals have always interested me more than organisations, institutions or teams. One of the lecturers who had a big influence on me at TCD was the Presbyterian minister Reverend Terence McCaughey. He was brought up on the Antrim Road in Belfast and, as a young fellow, used to go on holiday to Ballycastle, where he heard old men speaking Irish as they loaded cattle onto boats going over to Rathlin Island. That stimulated his interest in the language, in much the same way as the old man down at home, P.J. Campbell, had prompted mine. Terence went to Cambridge to study English, where he became friendly with Ted Hughes, who would go on to become Poet Laureate. They met in the first fortnight in university, roomed close to each other and remained lifelong friends. In fact, Hughes wrote practically every week to Terence. I visited my old lecturer in Rathfarnham in his later years. He was still wonderfully lucid, and meeting his wife, Ohna, of whom Terence had always spoken so lovingly, was a joy. Over a cup of tea, she told me that I had been in their kitchen for thirty years. 'Every time you came on the radio, Terence would stop everything and say, "Hold on, I want to hear what Eamonn is saying."' He was an independent thinker, a genuine Christian, a modest man and a man of courage. *Ar dheis Dé go raibh a anam.*

Many years ago, I spent some time tracing the background of the Northern Ireland civil rights movement. I went to see a man called Fred Heatley, who was the first secretary of the Civil Rights Association. During our conversation, he said, 'Did you know that the first cheque we ever got for the movement was from a Presbyterian minister?' I said to Fred, 'I will name that minister.' He could not believe it when I named Terence. He was astounded.

Another great influence on me in Trinity was Professor Nigel Glendinning. Although he was a Spanish lecturer, he opened my eyes not just to literature but to architecture, to humour and, above all, to art. I was also fortunate to get to know poet and lecturer Brendan Kennelly a little while I was at college, and more after I left. I wish I had done English, if for no other reason than to listen to Kennelly's mellifluous voice. Fellow poet and Trinity alumnus Michael Longley, who worked in a factory in England as a student with Kennelly, captures the very essence of Brendan in his poem 'The Factory for Brendan Kennelly': 'Talking too much, drowning me in his hurlygush, which makes the sound water makes over stones'.

How blessed I was to share, if only for a while, the same oasis as these two creative spirits. I was born into a poor family and Trinity College's doors opened to me. Years later, our daughters Ciara and Laura-Kate walked in my footsteps and, just recently, I heard with delight my little granddaughter Anna declare, 'I am going to Trinity.' I had a wonderful time there, 'and when I am dead, lay me down with Trinity colours at my head and feet'.

***

It was in Sloopy's Disco in D'Olier Street on 6 September 1971 that I met the young woman who would become my wife. I had just returned from Spain, where I had been teaching English for the summer and improving my Spanish. A college friend, Barry Gaughan, persuaded me to accompany him to the disco with the offer of free tickets. I was tanned, fresh-faced and wearing a red corduroy bomber jacket and clogs. When Detta is telling the story of our first meeting, she often says that she noticed my white teeth. Early in the evening, I spotted a beautiful girl with a sylph-like figure, big blue eyes and inky black hair, with two plaits in the style of Bo Derek's. Hot pants were all the rage at the time, and she was also wearing brown suede gladiator sandals. I kept my eye on her throughout the evening and finally made my move when the second-last set of dances was announced. That was the night Detta Costelloe entered my life, and she has been by my side ever since.

Back in the early days of our relationship, I used to joke with Detta about her dark Latin colouring, saying that perhaps her lineage could be traced back to some Spanish sailor who was shipwrecked off the west coast of Ireland in the sixteenth century. Nothing could be further from the truth, according to research into her family tree by her late uncle, who traced the Costelloes back to the Anglo-Normans of the twelfth century. Throughout my college days, Detta and I saw a lot of each other, made easier by the fact that she didn't work far away from Trinity. She had done a business course, specialising in computers, and was employed by one of Ireland's biggest civil engineering infrastructure companies, Public Works. I had a bicycle, and many a time in the early hours of the morning I cycled up Grafton Street with Detta on the crossbar, bringing her back to her apartment in Ranelagh. Back then we did a lot of freewheeling down the hill.

One less successful adventure was the night we went camping in the Dublin mountains. It was an unmitigated disaster. Because of the wind, I couldn't secure the pathetic little tent I had procured, and the rain was coming down like stair rods. That was the end of camping for us.

The incompetence I demonstrated that night has only got worse. My father had hands with which he could do anything. I cannot drive a nail straight. When it comes to doing anything about the house, I usually break whatever I touch. Detta is the practical half in our marriage. I am the one with the flights of fancy, but in a mere few words she brings me back down to earth.

In those days, relationships were a little more gradual – there was no moving in together after the first week. I didn't meet Detta's mother, Nora, until the second year of our courtship, and the meeting itself was quite a formal affair. She invited Detta and me for lunch at Wynn's, off O'Connell Street. Back then, Wynn's was a fashionable hotel, particularly popular with country people. A three-course lunch was not something to which I was accustomed. In fact, it might well have been the first three-course lunch I'd had in any hotel. Mrs Costelloe was a sophisticated, stylish lady. She came across as a well-travelled person of strong character. As you would expect, I was watching my Ps and Qs during that lunch – careful not to make 'a mouth of myself', as we say in South Armagh.

It was the following year when I received my official invitation to travel west to the Costelloe homestead in Tuam, County Galway. For any young man it is daunting to meet a partner's parents and siblings for the first time, and I was no different. The red carpet was rolled out for me, the best china was on show and the fatted calf was killed. On my first visit, we dined in the very room where our wedding reception would be held a few years later. That room was beautifully furnished with quality pieces that Mrs Costelloe had picked up over the years at auctions in old manses and parochial houses. I felt quite at home in the company of Mr Costelloe and Detta's brother, Paddy, with whom I had a genuine rapport from the outset. Having been reared on a small farm, I was familiar with farming parlance. Paddy went on to marry Kitty, who lights up every room into which she walks. Detta's older sister, Mary, was already married to Gerry by the time I met her. Mary was always a dote, sharing so many of my wife's best characteristics. From the get-go I always felt entirely comfortable in their company.

Detta's father, Michael, was a farmer, yes – but not what I expected. He was quite professorial in disposition, delighted to engage me in conversation about history – Irish, British and international. A recurring topic was the Anglo-Irish Trade War, better known as the Economic War, which was a trade war between Ireland and the UK that took place between 1932 and 1938. Both countries imposed unilateral trade restrictions, causing severe damage to the Irish economy. Mr Costelloe remembered bringing calves to the marketplace in the 1930s and coming home with another two or three animals that had been thrown into his cart or trailer because the market was dead and very poor farmers could not afford to feed the stock that hadn't sold. The policies of de Valera, responsible for the Economic War, shifted the political dial to Fine Gael in the Costelloe house, where it has remained to this day.

My arrival on the scene provided a new area of interest for Detta's father – the Troubles in Northern Ireland. He was fascinated by Ian Paisley. I wasn't ever long in the house before he would ask, 'How is big Paisley?'

***

I graduated from university in the summer of 1974, and then spent some time freelancing as a journalist. I continued living in Dublin that year. September of 1975 would prove an eventful month in my life. I was already planning to move back to Northern Ireland with a view to finding employment at the British Broadcasting Corporation (BBC). It was around that time I turned up at Detta's apartment in Ranelagh in the early hours of the morning, and when she opened the door I suggested to her that we should get engaged straight away and that we get should get married in January 1976. Thankfully she said yes to both proposals.

Detta and her family set about planning our wedding, which was set for 3 January 1976. January can be a wicked month in Ireland, but none of us had anticipated the fearsome storm that would batter Ireland the night before. I cannot recall anything comparable to the hurricane that raged that night. Family and friends travelling from Northern Ireland and Dublin to Galway had to battle against gale-force winds, lashing rain and roads blocked with fallen trees. It was simply horrendous. My father affectionately referred to it as a real 'Kitty the Hare' night. Kitty the Hare stories appeared in the *Our Boys* magazine that we read at home – her stories were firmly anchored in Ireland and given to much hyperbole.

Plans had been laid for our wedding reception to be held at Detta's family home. Caterers were coming to prepare the food at the house but, in the middle of that wild night, the transformer on the driveway caught fire, meaning there was no electricity. Everything for the wedding reception had to be rushed to the convent in Tuam to be cooked there.

We got married in the Costelloes' local church in Cortoon. Detta's uncle, Canon Paddy, officiated, assisted by Father Carter, the parish priest. The tempestuous storm the night before and the drama of the transformer going on fire in the driveway only served to heighten the excitement at the wedding reception.

It was a truly wonderful Irish wedding night of music, dance, song and craic. Detta and I eventually went to bed at 5 a.m.

***

In the early days of our relationship, Detta always told me she couldn't wait to get away from the farm, and that would still be her attitude today. She was made for living in the city – she loves the buzz. Boarding at Taylor's Hill Dominican College in Galway afforded her an opportunity to grow in independence, which made it easier for her to enjoy life in cities like Dublin and Belfast. Detta met my sister Goretti and her future husband, Tony, very early in our relationship as Goretti had moved to Dublin for work. Their close bond remains to this day. She met the wider Mallie family at the wedding of my older brother, Michael, in 1972. She shared a room on that visit to my parents' home with my two sisters, Carmel and Goretti, and did not sleep one wink the whole night, laughing and yo-hoing.

From the first day of my meeting Detta, it was clear that fashion was very important to her. I loved that then, and I still love it. She is very lucky because she would look well dressed in a meal bag – she would probably accessorise it with a big belt. Very early on, I also discovered in Detta a woman who was not impressed by people with money. Had she been, she would not have stayed with me. Money is not the yardstick she uses to measure the worth of someone. She is a woman of faith with an open mind. I just know that if I happened to give a person in the street a fiver, Detta would give that person a tenner.

She has always been low-key and subtle, but no one should

be fooled – there is steel in this lady. I witnessed this in recent years when she was hit with three bad bouts of illness, including breast cancer, which resulted in a mastectomy. Her pragmatic, sanguine approach in deciding to have her breast removed was something to behold. I stood looking on in awe of her courage as I listened to her exchanges with her consultant, at the end of which she calmly and almost casually told her, 'Okay, remove it.' As long as I have known Detta she has loved animals. We don't have a dog and it is just as well, because I am not sure how I would fare in a competition for her affections. In terms of loyalty, whether to her family or to her friends, she is 'as constant as the northern star'. From the get-go, she got on very well with my small circle of friends and acquaintances in college, feeling at home in that milieu.

About twenty-five years ago, Detta and I were guests at a dinner at Hillsborough Castle. Couples were split up for the meal – I ended up at one end of the table and Detta was at the other. A journalist sitting opposite her – not known to her – asked her, 'Why did you marry him?', nodding towards me further down the table. Detta treated the question as a joke and changed the subject, but the man asked it again. She replied, 'From the first time I met Eamonn, I didn't know what he was going to do next, and I still don't know.' He then added, 'Eamonn Mallie is an enigma. I suppose he chased you.' 'No,' replied Detta, 'I chased him.' That shut him up (although it was not true). 'That's my girl. I'm so proud of you,' I said later that evening.

Chapter Three

Doubling Down on Discrimination

WHEN I LEFT TRINITY College in the summer of 1974, I had no clear direction of travel in terms of a career. I had studied Spanish and Irish, thanks to my romantic leanings – I love all languages without prejudice. I had notions about broadcasting on radio and television, but this was informed by nothing more than vanity.

After university, I applied for a job as a newsreader at RTÉ and despite my not getting that post, someone suggested I should be accommodated in the company. A research opportunity arose in radio for a freelancer who spoke Irish to work in the current affairs and features department. I started working for a decent man called Pádraig Dolan. In programme-making, ideas flow from the producer, the editor and the researcher. It was my job to tease out the respective facts of the story from every perspective, mindful of the importance of editorial accuracy. Naturally, I wanted a full-time, salaried post. I learned that being a full member of the National Union of Journalists (NUJ) would be to my advantage, but I found my application blocked for no apparent reason.

Realising that I was in something of a cul-de-sac, career-wise, I applied for a post as a trainee radio current affairs producer at the BBC in Belfast. When I told my family that I was going for the job, my aunt Minnie, who was the well-travelled and educated one in our family, received the news with disbelief, warning me that the BBC would not give a job to a Catholic from South Armagh. She thought that I should become a teacher instead. I had been teaching English in Barcelona and in other parts of Spain over four summers. The work had paid well, but I knew enough about myself to know that I didn't want to follow that career path. I told my aunt that I appreciated what she said, but that I was going to test my employment prospects with the BBC.

I was called for an interview with the BBC in Ormeau Avenue in September 1975, just after Detta and I had become engaged. When I boarded the train to Belfast, it was so busy that there was only one free seat that I could take. It turned out to be next to David Hammond, the larger-than-life folk singer, BBC producer and filmmaker. On David's other side was the actor Michael Duffy, who came from Crossmaglen in South Armagh. Cheered by such good company on the train, I felt that I acquitted myself reasonably well in front of the BBC board, but one person seemed hostile. I wondered whether my aunt's worst fears would be realised. At the end of the interview, I was asked if I had any questions. I decided to put the buck to the brae: 'Will the BBC give someone of my background a job?' I asked. There was an embarrassing silence for what felt like a long time. Robin Walsh, who was a member of the board and the head of news at the BBC, leant across the table, pointed his finger at me and said, 'If we want you, boy, we will take you.' I got the job and I was scarcely through the door when I got my NUJ membership card.

I got to know Walsh while I was at the BBC. He was one of the finest journalists I have ever known; someone with outstanding editorial judgement. He took no prisoners. I only wish I'd had an opportunity to have worked under him. I started as a trainee producer at *Good Morning Ulster*, Radio Ulster's flagship breakfast news programme. My experience there was not very edifying, but what *was* edifying was the fact that I was sent off to London to do my training. It was there I discovered my calling. In the course of the training, like everybody else, I was dispatched to do an interview in the city. When I returned to the training centre, the course leaders devoted more time to my technique than to anyone else's. My aptitude for interviewing was underscored in the report they sent to Belfast about me.

The first story I covered for the BBC was a very unusual one. Late one evening during my early days there, Terry Sharkey, the producer of *Good Morning Ulster* and a very good journalist, came over to my desk and dropped a cutting in front of me. It was a death notice, thumbnail size, from the *News Letter*. Terry said, 'Will you look at that and then take a race up to the house and see what it's about?'

The death notice went like something like this: 'Doole. In the presence of Her Majesty the Queen, Tuesday November 6. In the presence of his Highness the King, Wednesday November 7. House private.' The address was in the Shankill Road area, so I called a taxi. I didn't know Belfast at all and now I was headed for a strictly Protestant area. So, yes, I was nervous. I was from South Armagh.

When I knocked on the door, a portly little man opened it. I told him who I was and he invited me in. He was a gentleman. He explained to me the background to the death notice. He had been responsible for keeping the boilers running at Daisy Hill Hospital in Newry throughout the Ulster Workers' Council strike in 1974 and he was decorated by the Queen for his services. Being unmarried, he'd decided to bring his elderly mother with him to Buckingham Palace. She'd died the next day. He graciously agreed to an interview, which was broadcast on Radio Ulster.

My first encounter with violence as a reporter was on my own doorstep at home in South Armagh when loyalists shot up and bombed Donnelly's Bar in Silverbridge, which was the hub of our local community. My sister Goretti had worked in the bar when she was still at school. Radio Ulster sent me to report from there. Three civilians were killed in that attack on 19 December 1975: the owners' 14-year-old son, known to us as Wee Michael Donnelly, along with 35-year-old Trevor Bracknell and 24-year-old Patrick Donnelly (no relation to the owners). These killings weighed heavily on my parents since they were very good friends of Marie and Gerry Donnelly, who lost their young son that night. For me, having until recently led a charmed existence as a student and university graduate in Dublin, it was a rough reintroduction to life in Northern Ireland.

Dozens were also injured in the Donnelly's Bar attack, including a friend of my dad, Gerry Carragher, who lost his leg. I regularly visited Gerry in the Royal Victoria Hospital, and during one of my conversations with him he casually said to me, 'I'm going to get the spare wheel fitted tomorrow.' This was a reference to his artificial leg. Despite the bleakness of his situation, the human spirit won through.

Just a month after the events in Silverbridge, following our wedding in January 1976, I brought my new bride to live in Belfast, in a rented apartment in Stranmillis. Detta had no job when she first arrived but was keen to start work. Lady Luck struck when she was having her hair done in a salon near our home and the elegant woman next to her engaged her in conversation. That woman was Carole Neill, and her husband, Bobby, was looking for a private secretary. Detta went to work for the Neills, owners of finance company CRN.

Two or three weeks into our marriage, our apartment was rocked when a device exploded in a house a few doors down. It's thought a workman pushed open a door to check an electric meter. A bomb detonated and he was badly injured. This was not a great introduction to Belfast for a new wife. Thankfully, though, Detta readily made Belfast her home and has often said she wouldn't ever leave the city in which we have brought up our children.

Around the same time, I was back home, visiting my family in South Armagh. My brother Anthony wanted to go to Cullyhanna to pick up a television that he was having repaired there and I agreed to drive him. Peadar, my younger brother, joined us for the spin. As we drew near Cullyhanna, we were met with an army checkpoint. Inexplicably, the soldiers took me from my car and frogmarched me into the village. One of the soldiers handed the keys of my car to my brothers and instructed them to drive home.

I could not believe my eyes when I saw the highly respected local headmaster, Hugh Macauley (father of RTÉ Northern Ireland correspondent Conor Macauley), also being marched into the village. In fact, every male from that immediate area had been rounded up. We were lined up in a row in the village centre, with no idea what was going on. The soldiers were using Labrador sniffer dogs to check us for traces of explosives. Two brothers, well-known local wildfowlers, who were always out shooting ducks and pheasants, appeared in the village with their dogs. The army Labradors lost all interest in us and immediately set about sniffing around the two new dogs on the scene. Privately, we had a good laugh at that.

The army then marched a number of us up into the grounds of Cullyhanna church and out into a field beyond, where a helicopter was waiting. A soldier told us to get into the chopper and it lifted off. There was worse to come. When we came close to Bessbrook, which would turn out to be our destination, the pilot decided to engage in some aerobatics, nose-diving from a great height over the water in Camlough Lake. It was a terrifying experience.

We then landed at the military base, originally a linen mill, in Bessbrook, where we were instructed to stand up straight and to stare into a quarry. I was eventually brought into an office for questioning. I was asked for some details about myself and what I did for a living. When I told the soldiers I was a journalist and produced my NUJ card, my feet did not hit the ground. I was out the gate immediately. I called our family friend Jim McAvoy, who came and brought me home. It was a very instructive experience for me to have as a journalist – an insight into how totally innocent people must feel when they find themselves so unfairly treated.

***

The first political story I broke in my time at the BBC was the resignation of British Prime Minister Harold Wilson on 16 March 1976. I had been monitoring Downtown Radio, the new commercial radio station in Northern Ireland, and they had flashed the news. When I bumped into W.D. Flackes, the political editor, and told him about Wilson's resignation, he was shocked – both because the news was such a bolt from the blue and because it was coming to him courtesy of this whippersnapper who had just arrived on the scene. His response was 'Oh good Lord, where did you hear that?'

I found working in BBC Radio Ulster a little oppressive and parochial, perhaps because I had spent the previous four years in Dublin and had been back and forward to Europe regularly. I was forced to stare reality in the face. When I walked into the *Good Morning Ulster* office, I got the impression I produced a certain frisson of disquiet. I simply felt a bit of a 'spare' about the place. Apart from Paul Clarke, Gloria Hunniford and some of the secretaries who worked in Radio Ulster, no one else reached out to me. Yes, I exuded an air of confidence, and some might have interpreted this as a cockiness. I didn't endear myself to others when I won a black-and-white portable television in a BBC Club draw very soon after my arrival in Ormeau Avenue. There were those who begrudged me that television a lot. It was as if I had won it without buying a ticket for the draw. To this day, I still get the odd jibe about winning that TV, making me feel like the interloper who stole it.

My head of department, Dan Gilbert, had silenced my voice in the shaping of programme output. I was live to events in the Republic of Ireland and beyond, but each time I proposed a story, he shot me down with the riposte 'It has been done before, dear boy.' Quite often I had to point out that it hadn't been done before; that it had, in fact, just happened. He did not give me a favourable midterm report during my probation period, so I resigned. Getting a job at the BBC had been difficult in the first place, but extricating myself was even more so. After informing Dan that I was quitting, I went to see Bob Pugh, the head of administration, to tell him that I was resigning. There was no chance of my leaving that afternoon – when you joined the BBC in those days, you were expected to stay until retirement, and I had to go through quite a bureaucratic rigmarole to get out.

Downtown Radio had started broadcasting on 16 March 1976 and I was listening regularly. It sounded fresh, friendly and airy in tone. It put a big emphasis on frequency of news, with headlines every half hour and news on the hour. It broke the mould in Northern Ireland. When something happened, it was verified and then put straight on air. That's why there was a huge listenership – the constant flow of information and news. As a result, it was my next natural port of call. I made my way there to meet the head of news, Louis Kelly. The minute I walked into the newsroom, I felt at home: the atmosphere was electric. I was given a reporter's job without pomp or ceremony – I hadn't even filled in an application form.

Once there, I was introduced to Maurice Hawkins, a news editor. Maurice is one of the most brilliant wordsmiths I have ever met, a man who can say the same thing a hundred different ways – a gift to any editor. He is left-wing, a trade unionist and a good Ballycarry Protestant. He and I hit it off the first day we met. Unfortunately, not all my new colleagues were so welcoming – very quickly I discovered considerable hostility in the newsroom. There were at least five people who either did not take to me or didn't like me at all. Perhaps it was something in me – in my personality, in my character – that provoked that reaction. I know I had an air of unjustifiable arrogance about me, either due to insecurity or innate confidence. I haven't yet worked that out. Perhaps the fact that I was a Catholic was an issue for them. I was also the only graduate in that newsroom and maybe I was resented for that reason. However, I took some comfort from the fact that there were also those who respected me, admired me and stood by me.

The first serious shot across my bows came when I was called upstairs to the office of the managing director, David Hannon. There I was accused of having handed untreated copy to the news desk for on-air broadcasting. This accusation was totally without foundation – I'd had nothing to do with the copy in question and hadn't ever seen it, let alone handed it to anyone. Hannon's follow-up remark was insulting: 'I think we have bought a pup instead of a dog.' I determined to show that man that I had a bite.

There came a point, though, less than six months after I'd started at Downtown, when the pressure was considerable and the hostility towards me escalated. As well as being ignored, snide remarks about me were commonplace in exchanges between two particular journalists. The atmosphere was poisonous, the tension unbearable for me. I drafted my resignation. I went upstairs and handed it to the fair-minded programme controller, Don Anderson. He read it and said, 'Eamonn, you are going nowhere. I believe in you.' Don explained that he had been a teacher, hated teaching and had gone to work for the Belfast *News Letter*. One of the journalists on the desk always referred to him as 'the failed teacher'. Don decided to prove that man wrong and ended up an international reporter for the BBC. He told me, 'Go downstairs, put your head down, do your work and you will rise above them all.' I took his advice and will always be grateful to him.

The hostility towards me didn't stop, but Maurice Hawkins, who was head of the NUJ in the station, stood up at a meeting and announced that he was making me his deputy in the Downtown Radio chapel. From that day onwards it was Maurice and I who did all the negotiating with management on behalf of everybody in the newsroom. This changed everything – it afforded me standing and a sphere of influence.

***

Early in my time in Downtown Radio, I arrived home from work and told Detta that I had to go to Banbridge that night to interview and record Enoch Powell, the South Down Ulster Unionist MP. I'd been out working so many nights on the run since starting at Downtown that I suggested to Detta that she join me rather than spending another night on her own at home, and she agreed.

We arrived at the Orange Hall in Banbridge, but the locals wouldn't let us into the building. I was Eamonn Mallie – I wasn't getting in, full stop. My name told them everything. When Enoch Powell arrived, I explained my problem to him. He turned to his followers and said, 'Gentlemen, gentlemen, we need the press. We need to be heard. Come ahead, come ahead.' Detta and I went into the hall and sat down. I was so nervous. It was my first big political marking. I had brought two tape recorders and two microphones, fearing that just one tape might run out.

As Powell was addressing the Orange brotherhood, he spotted that I was engaged in something – in fact, I was switching from one tape to the next. He looked down at me and said, 'Are you in pain?' I replied, 'No, I'm okay, sir.' 'Shall we continue?' he asked. 'Yes, carry on,' I replied.

Powell was an enigma. Here was a man with one of the finest minds in Britain, who could command the attention of the entire House of Commons. He was potentially 'the best Prime Minister Britain never had', but the 'Rivers of Blood' speech that he gave in 1968 – which was deeply offensive and in which he criticised mass immigration – guaranteed that he had no future in the Conservative Party. (At the time of the speech, he was the party's shadow secretary of state for defence.)

He ended up a political outcast, who, in 1974, found a home in the UUP and wielded very considerable influence over the party leader, Jim Molyneaux. I abhorred his utterances about migrants, but I couldn't help but admire his erudition and learnedness as a classicist and an orator.

Powell held the view that Northern Ireland was under-represented proportionately at Westminster. In 1978, he proposed a Speaker's Conference, the aim of which was to establish whether Northern Ireland had the appropriate number of MPs. Powell was successful and secured greater representation at Westminster for Northern Ireland. When he turned up at the next UUP annual conference, there was uproar because his promotion of increased representation had ironically resulted in more nationalist MPs (from the SDLP) at Westminster. The party members resented that his actions had increased the representation of nationalists at Westminster and complained about it. Powell boldly stood up and said, 'Ladies and gentlemen, that's democracy; that's democracy.' That was not what his audience wanted to hear – but this is what made him such a compelling politician. He was in a different class. He had style. I really admired his courage. He was a rarity. His appeal to me says something about my own make-up. I always gravitate towards people who do not conform to the norm. I am a bit like that myself.

As a reporter at Downtown Radio, I was effectively a fire-man: always at the ready – day and night – to cover whatever was happening across Northern Ireland. The phone was liable to ring at any hour. On 17 February 1978, I was at home when the news desk rang to tell me that a bomb had exploded at the La Mon House Hotel in County Down. As I made my way there from our South Belfast home, out across the Castlereagh Hills, I could not have prepared myself for the horror that awaited me.

I was the first journalist on the scene. When I arrived, a police officer called George Morrison, who came into Downtown regularly, took me to a vantage point from where I could see the scale of the inferno. I witnessed the charred body of a woman, face down, being removed from the carnage. We learned later that the IRA had planted a large incendiary device containing a napalm-like substance on the windowsill of the restaurant. Twelve people were killed, several burnt alive, and thirty were injured. They were nearly all members of the Irish Collie Club and the Northern Ireland Junior Motorcycle Club, holding their annual dinner dances in the Peacock Room and Gransha Room respectively. I was fortunate that night that Ivan Little was duty editor on the news desk in Downtown – his presence eased my burden somewhat as Ivan had vast experience as a journalist, having covered the Troubles for years. He had good editorial judgement and respected my capacity and commitment to my work. Furthermore, he was technically adroit and could turn audio reports around very quickly. He knew his business and we worked well together.

My experience of the La Mon atrocity would be the first of many similar atrocities over the next twenty years. Edna O'Brien called one of her books *August is a Wicked Month*. That was certainly true of August 1979 on the island of Ireland. I was in the Downtown newsroom when we received a call from a journalist in Sligo informing us that Lord Mountbatten's boat had been bombed while out at sea near Mullaghmore. I drove like a madman all the way to Mullaghmore, a journey of three or four hours. The scene there was surreal. It was a glorious evening – the sun glistening on the vast expanse of waters in Donegal Bay – but a cloud of sadness had descended on the village. Lord Mountbatten and members of his family were familiar faces there, spending their summers at Classiebawn Castle, overlooking the Atlantic Ocean. We soon learned that the IRA had triggered a bomb that had blown up Mountbatten's fishing boat, *Shadow V*, killing him, members of his family and Enniskillen schoolboy Paul Maxwell. The teenager helped on the boat each summer. In those days, there were no mobile phones, so I was dependent on the generosity of a local person who allowed me to use her phone to report to my desk in Belfast and further afield.

More would follow that day. In a typical South Armagh IRA operation, paramilitaries had planted two bombs at different points at Narrow Water Castle on the outskirts of Warrenpoint in South Down. A British Army convoy, consisting of a Land

Rover and two lorries travelling from Ballykinlar to Newry, took the force of the first explosion. An 800lb fertiliser bomb had been concealed in bales of straw in a parked truck on the Warrenpoint to Newry side of the road. Six members of the Parachute Regiment died in that explosion. When reinforcements arrived at the scene, they gathered in the entrance to Narrow Water Castle on the opposite side of the road but, unknown to them, the IRA's second 800lb bomb was waiting for them. It was remotely detonated, killing twelve soldiers: ten from the Parachute Regiment and two from the Queen's Own Highlanders. Among those killed was Lieutenant Colonel Blair, one of two of the highest-ranking soldiers to die in the Troubles up to that point. That double bomb attack would turn out to be the deadliest assault on the British Army during the Troubles. A civilian also died when shots were fired by soldiers, who had mistaken him for a terrorist, across the lough.

When I arrived at Narrow Water after a long drive from Mullaghmore, I could only compare what met me to a scene from a war film, with debris and parts of the vehicles in which the soldiers had been travelling strewn all over the road. Despite the grotesqueness of those killings that day, like many of my fellow journalists I was, by then, almost inured to these events, which resulted in empty chairs in homes right across these islands. No one back then could have foreseen a day when the killings would stop.

When the Irish National Liberation Army (INLA) planted a bomb on 6 December 1982 at a bar known as the Dropping Well in Ballykelly, County Derry, I found myself there covering the story for seventeen hours. The bomb killed eleven soldiers and six civilians. While I was at the scene, Defence Secretary

John Nott arrived and, during his visit, he gave me an interview. As he was being whisked away in his armour-plated vehicle, I discovered that I had not recorded a single word of what he had said. I told my journalist colleague and friend Deric Henderson to jump into my Land Rover – the car helped us to blend into Nott's convoy as it headed for the airport. I drove in under the blades of his helicopter and persuaded the minister to do another interview. It was all quite reckless – we could have been shot dead by the police or the army when we joined the convoy or when we approached the helicopter.

More often than not, the violence was less than a stone's throw away from my home in South Belfast. Unionist MP Robert Bradford lived a few streets away from me and, for work, I had been in his home a number of times. I was always made welcome. On 14 November 1981, he was shot dead by the IRA at a community centre in Finaghy, not far from where we both lived. I raced to the scene. Robert's body was scarcely cold when I got there. Having become acquainted with both him and his wife, Norah, over the years, his killing had a real impact on me.

Another Ulster Unionist I knew who was killed was Edgar Graham, a law lecturer at Queen's University. I had spent quite a lot of time in his company and he struck me as an intelligent and very civilised person. He had publicly supported supergrass trials, in which paramilitaries testified against their former comrades in court in return for clemency. The trials were hugely controversial, especially because they were heard by one judge sitting alone, usually wearing a bulletproof vest. Graham was shot dead by the IRA outside Queen's University Belfast on 7 December 1983. He was still a young man, one who didn't get a chance to live his life.

I also vividly recall the 1984 murder of William McConnell, who was assistant governor at the Maze Prison. Just after he was killed, I travelled to his home in Hawthornden Drive, East Belfast, to report on the shooting. Three weeks earlier, I had done an interview with William – the only interview he had ever done up until then – and I introduced him to Independent Television News (ITN) to do an interview as well. I often wonder if I hadn't done that interview with Mr McConnell, would he still be alive? That still concerns me. Years later, I still had a photograph on my desk of the youthful McConnell in his graduation gown.

∗∗∗

The day that Detta called me at work and told me she was expecting a baby, Maurice Hawkins looked down the table at me after I'd hung up and said, 'Detta's pregnant.' I hadn't said anything to give it away – he just read me well. I could not contain myself. I was presenting a farming programme on Downtown Radio on the day the baby arrived, 23 May 1978. The programme was coming live from the Balmoral Show in South Belfast. D.J. Hendi was running the radio desk for me, and during my broadcast he opened his microphone and announced to all the world that Detta had just given birth to a baby girl. He asked any listeners who were at the show to make their way to the outside-broadcast desk if they had any suggestions for a name. A lady approached me later and asked, 'What do you think of the name Ciara?' I loved it and I raced to the Royal Victoria Hospital to ask Detta what she thought. She was equally keen, and our little girl was christened Ciara.

Our next child arrived on 30 August 1980. Detta suddenly felt that the baby was coming, so I got her into the car and we headed for the City Hospital, which was thankfully very close by. We arrived at Jubilee Maternity in the nick of time and Laura-Kate was born. Our son, Michael, was born three years later, on 10 February 1983. His arrival completed the new Mallie–Costelloe family and we gave Michael his mum's family surname as a middle name out of respect for the Costelloes.

Detta had been educated in a homogeneous Catholic schooling environment in Galway; Northern Ireland was anything but homogeneous when it came to education. She believed strongly that primary school should provide a religious foundation for the children, so they all went to St Bride's, which was near our house. For secondary school, they went on to State schools. We have no regrets about those decisions. The girls went to Victoria, which had a wonderful pastoral dimension to it, and Ciara and Laura-Kate on balance were very happy there.

Michael went to Methodist College (Methody). He'd already played mini rugby for Instonians at Shane Park, and he continued to play at school. His rugby at Pirrie Park (Methody's rugby grounds) gave me endless pleasure – I watched him every Saturday morning for seven years. The journeys there weren't always the happiest – he'd often forgotten one of his boots or his blazer – but I'll say no more about that!

Michael McCormick, who owned Murphy's Butchers on the Lisburn Road, fed all the young fellows like Michael on Saturday mornings with Guinness sausages cooked on the barbecue outside his store. Coming up to a Schools' Cup final, McCormick put a proposition to our Michael: 'If Methody wins, and if you wear the Murphy's Butchers cap at the end of the game, I'll give you a hundred pounds.' After the team had won, Michael ran to the changing room, emerged with the cap on him and in every photograph taken that day he is wearing it. Michael McCormick, being the honourable man that he is, paid up.

It was no accident that there were sporting genes in our children. Detta's cousins all played GAA and her cousin Enda Colleran particularly distinguished himself as the captain of the famous Galway county team that won three All-Irelands in a row. My own family was steeped in GAA and various other sports, such as soccer and golf. Detta distinguished herself as a runner and netball player. Laura-Kate played hockey at Victoria College, while Ciara opted for cross-country running. Tennis and horse riding figured heavily in the lives of all our children, along with music and the Young Lyric theatre, which the children would deem to be the most important part of their education in terms of how it prepared them for life after school, when it came to going for jobs and presenting their case.

Our home was rarely silent, with the clarinet playing here, the piano playing there and so on. We gained inestimable pleasure from the girls' involvement in choral singing and school productions. I doubt if there is a song from a contemporary musical of which Laura-Kate doesn't know the words. Nothing gives Detta and me more joy than to watch Ciara and Laura-Kate now following the same musical path with their own children, Kate, Anna, Rory, Eve and Ríain.

Those were wonderful years. I am still friendly with some of the fathers from Michael's rugby days, and those young men from all backgrounds with whom he played rugby are still part of our family. Similarly with the girls, their friends in many cases are our friends. Detta had an open-door policy – she always loved young people coming to the house. Detta and I had no special formula about how the children should be brought up, but we didn't ever chase them away from the tea table or the dinner table when adults arrived. We tried to include them and to integrate them into every part of our lives. The girls have grown up as mirror images of their mum in their passion for family, fun, music, laughter, gregariousness and faith.

After studying property in Newcastle upon Tyne, Michael worked for Savills Commercial in London before training as a primary school teacher. He then joined me at Mallie Media, our documentary-making company. He has broken new ground in the industry to which I introduced him – he was one of two producers of the film *Nothing Compares* about Sinéad O'Connor, which premiered at the Sundance Film Festival on 2 January 2022.

However, if you want to be at the top of your game or among the best, journalism is a selfish profession. I cannot deny that my success came at a price – sometimes at the expense of my family. The drive to succeed often took me away from the dinner table and away from my wife and children. Quite recently Detta told me, 'There were times I didn't know where you went or where you were. You could have been dead.' That was true – that was the sort of life I lived. I could not have done it without Detta, but looking at my own daughters now, the way I lived would not be tolerated today by young women and mothers – and rightly so.

Chapter Four

Bobby Sands

DURING MY FIRST TRIP to Spain, when I was teaching English in San Sebastián in 1970, a neighbour asked me about Terence MacSwiney. I'd learned about Zwingli, Calvin and Papal Bulls from the Christian Brothers in Abbey Grammar, but I had not been taught Irish history. I had scarcely heard of MacSwiney, the playwright, author and politician who was elected as Sinn Féin lord mayor of Cork in 1920. He was arrested by the British government on charges of sedition and sentenced to two years in jail, to be served in Brixton Prison. He died there on 25 October 1920 after a seventy-four-day hunger strike. His death attracted interest around the world and brought the Irish republican campaign against the British presence in Ireland to international attention. That death would strike a chord again on the island of Ireland in 1980, when members of the IRA went on hunger strike in the Maze Prison.

In March 1976, Merlyn Rees, the secretary of state for Northern Ireland, had announced that anyone convicted of terrorist offences would no longer be entitled to special category status. Special category status had meant that the prisoners did not have to wear uniforms or do prison work; that they were housed with fellow members of their paramilitary group; and that they were allowed extra visits and food parcels. In September 1976, West Belfast man Kieran Nugent, a member of the IRA, was the first person to be jailed under this new regime. I knew Nugent, a ginger-haired man who was built like a tank and who had determination written all over his face. He said, 'If they want me to wear a uniform, they'll have to nail it to my back.' When Nugent refused to wear the uniform, he wasn't offered any other clothes, so he wrapped himself in a blanket, marking the beginning of the 'blanket protest'. Two years later, the 'no-wash' or 'dirty' protest kicked in, when the prisoners refused to leave their cells to slop out, and instead smeared excrement on the walls of their cells.

One of the biggest controversies during the IRA prisoners' protest in the Maze flowed from a visit by Cardinal Tomás Ó Fiaich on 30 July 1978. The statement he made forty-eight hours later was deemed explosive. 'Having spent the whole of Sunday in the prison I was shocked by the inhuman conditions prevailing in H Blocks 3, 4 and 5, where over 300 prisoners are incarcerated. One would hardly allow an animal to remain in such conditions, let alone a human being. The nearest approach to it that I have seen was the spectacle of hundreds of homeless people living in the sewer pipes in the slums of Calcutta.'

The graphic language used by one of the most senior figures in the Catholic Church in Ireland shocked even journalists like me. Prior to his intervention, the picture in the media and the public was governed by republican accounts of what was going on in the jail, which were viewed with some scepticism. Up until that point, we had no independent evidence of what life was like there and none of us could possibly have imagined the grotesqueness of the environment.

Political unionism was shocked and outraged at the directness of Ó Fiaich's statement. The British media had a field day in their attacks on the cardinal. Ian Paisley branded him 'the IRA bishop from Crossmaglen'. In fact, Ó Fiaich was 'as constant as the Northern Star' in his opposition to the IRA's violence. He once said of a united Ireland, 'The only unity worth having is a unity of hearts.'

Prime Minister Margaret Thatcher and Cardinal Ó Fiaich met in Downing Street on a number of occasions, and he shared with me the content of one exchange he had with her. He said she spoke about the British having good relations with Germany 'today'. Cardinal Ó Fiaich said, 'I suggested that perhaps the reason that the Germans are now friends with you is because the British are no longer in occupation of Germany.'

Each time Ó Fiaich travelled to London, he stayed with his English counterpart, Cardinal Basil Hume. Despite the camaraderie between the two men, they fundamentally disagreed on the morality of dying on hunger strike. Ó Fiaich told me, 'I don't believe it was suicide. I don't believe any person who goes on hunger strike, if he believes in his cause, I don't believe he could commit suicide, because in order to gain a victory he has to achieve at least part of what he went on hunger strike for, and then he comes off the hunger strike and that is always his hope. If you like, it is a little bit like dicing with death almost.'

***

A year after Ó Fiaich's visit, I too was in the Maze Prison, but in my case it was to meet with a member of the UVF, as well as with a member of the IRA, to try to understand why the protests were continuing and why cells were being wrecked. I spent a considerable time talking to a Portadown loyalist, whom I found to be very civilised and very informative. I was then brought to meet a prisoner called Roibeárd Ó Seachnasaigh – Bobby Sands – a republican. I knew nothing about him, nothing of his background. I was not even familiar with his name. My conversation with Ó Seachnasaigh lasted about an hour and was conducted in Irish. No one I have met who learned Irish in prison has had the competency that Sands had in articulating himself. I challenged him on the morality of the IRA killing of Earl Mountbatten and others at Mullaghmore earlier that year. His response was uncompromising: 'He knew what the Irish problem was. He did nothing about it. He came here every year to holiday and to enjoy this country.' Sands showed absolutely no remorse or empathy for Earl Mountbatten or the other people in that boat who were killed.

Little did I know that Sands would go on to become one of the best-known Irish republicans in the world. My meeting left me with a pitiful image of him. He was well into the no-wash protest by that stage, and the outworking of it was written all over his face. He was emaciated and gaunt, with long greasy hair, and his eyes were most unsettling and striking. They darted everywhere, as though he couldn't focus on me – perhaps as a result of the amount of time he had spent in isolation or because he was living in fear. I didn't get a chance to probe him about that. He was the antithesis of the smiling, healthy-looking young man in the murals in republican areas.

I later got to know members of the Sands family, including Bobby's sister Marcella and his parents. They were gentle people who ended up in a set of circumstances that they could not possibly have foreseen and the impact of what was happening to their son in the Maze was visible on their faces.

There was a sequel to that visit to the Maze. During my encounter with Sands, our speaking Irish had triggered something of a flap among the prison wardens. Suddenly they were scurrying all over the place, desperate – I assumed – to find someone who might understand what we were saying. Almost ten years later, I was attending a special UUP conference in Belfast when a big man approached me and greeted me with these words: 'I remember you from when you used to carry messages for the IRA into the Maze. You came in to see Bobby Sands. I was a prison officer in the jail then.' This man's allegation left me momentarily speechless and was clearly a defamation of my character. I invited that individual to come with me and repeat what he had just said in the presence of anybody in that hall. Of course, he didn't. I felt absolutely demeaned by his charge. The allegation levelled against me by that former prison officer illustrated how dangerous perception can be.

On 27 October 1980, republicans embarked on a hunger strike, which started with seven inmates of the Maze. Brendan Hughes, the Provisional IRA's commanding officer in the prison, was first to go on a 'no food' protest, and he was followed by another six men: Raymond McCartney, Tommy McKearney, Tommy McFeely, Leo Green and Sean McKenna of the IRA, and John Nixon of the INLA. They had five demands:

1. The right not to wear the prison uniform.
2. The right not to do prison work.
3. The right of free association with other prisoners, and to organise educational and recreational pursuits.
4. The right to one visit, one letter and one parcel a week.
5. Full restoration of remission lost during the protest.

On 1 December, three female prisoners in Armagh Prison – Mary Doyle, Mairéad Farrell and Mairéad Nugent – joined the strike. On 12 December, the loyalists joined in, with six UDA prisoners looking for the same five demands, with one addition: to be separated from republican prisoners. On 15 December, twenty-three republican prisoners joined the original seven hunger strikers; a day later a further seven became involved. On 17 December, Cardinal Ó Fiaich called on the strikers to end their protest and the UDA prisoners did so; a day later, so did the republicans. Controversy surrounded this event, as some republicans claimed to have a document from the British government setting out proposals to meet many of their demands, yet this did not happen.

As leader of the protesting prisoners, Sands was devastated that the British had won the battle and became determined that if another strike was planned, he would lead it and go all the way to death. And so it was that five years to the day since the special category status had been abolished, on 1 March 1981 Bobby Sands began the second republican hunger strike. He would be followed by twenty-three others, who started one by one, at intervals, for maximum propaganda value. Few years ripped community life apart more than that year, and I worked practically day and night during that awful time.

On 26 March, it was announced that Sands would contest the Fermanagh and South Tyrone by-election, which had come about because of the sudden death of independent MP Frank Maguire. I had always been curious about the identity of the person who had come up with the idea that Sands should stand in that by-election. It was only recently that former Sinn Féin Director of Publicity Danny Morrison told me that it was Jim Gibney, a former prisoner himself, who had suggested to him that Sands should stand. There followed a meeting in Monaghan of republican *cumainn* (societies) from along the border. The motion that Sands should stand was not passed. However, according to Morrison, scores of people making their way to the Monaghan meeting had been stopped by an Ulster Defence Regiment (UDR) patrol and held up for so long that the first vote had already happened by the time they arrived. Gerry Adams argued that a second vote should take place because there were so many latecomers. The second vote gave the green light. On 9 April 1981, Sands was elected.

The night the polls closed in the Fermanagh and South Tyrone by-election, June Gawley invited me for a drink with other journalists in Ulster Unionist Party headquarters in Enniskillen. I ended up in conversation with Harry West (the UUP candidate) and his wife, Maureen. I always liked Harry. His opening remark took me by surprise: 'I never thought the decent people of Fermanagh and South Tyrone would vote for the gunman.' In the course of our conversation, I asked him, 'Do you think there will ever be a United Ireland?' He went silent, but Maureen said, 'Well, Eamonn, it may come, but not through the barrel of a gun.' Harry piped up and said to his wife, 'Now, Mum, you're tiddly. Stay quiet.' I felt as though Maureen was letting the cat out of the bag about what was being said within the four walls of the West home.

* * *

Not in the history of my covering the Troubles in Northern Ireland did any event attract so much international news attention as the hunger strikes. There were days when I did as many as twenty broadcasts for stations all over the world, such was the fascination with the idea of prisoners starving themselves to death for political reasons. Having read some of Bobby Sands' writings and knowing about his awareness of international poets and literature, I often wonder what the same man might have done with his life in a different set of circumstances. Clearly, he was an intelligent individual.

Bobby Sands died on 5 May 1981. The Northern Ireland Office (NIO) statement said, 'Mr Robert Sands, prisoner in the Maze Prison, died today at 1.17 a.m. He took his own life by refusing food and medical intervention for 66 days.' Nine more republican prisoners died on that hunger strike and those involved ultimately revolutionised republican politics electorally, not just in Northern Ireland but also in the Republic of Ireland.

Republicans were master propagandists. The funerals of the hunger strikers were major spectacles, configured to facilitate foreign camera crews and reporters as much as possible. Where needed, scaffolding was erected so that photographers and camera operators could get the best angles. Graveside orations were recorded and broadcast around the world. Each funeral was meticulously choreographed, with family members walking in lockstep behind the coffin. Jimmy Drumm, a senior republican, was a central figure in the whole ritual surrounding the funerals – Father Denis Faul satirically referred to him as the 'minister for funerals'.

There was an endless cat-and-mouse game between the organisers of the funerals and the security services. The fact that a volley of shots was fired over the coffins of some of the hunger strikers put the police in difficult territory in deciding how to deal with these extraordinary circumstances, particularly because of the scale of the crowds attending the funerals. Normally, a helicopter buzzed overhead. I can still hear the report of the gunshots ringing in my ears as I stood beside Raymond McCreesh's coffin in Carrickcruppen graveyard in South Armagh. People from all over the island of Ireland turned up for these funerals, often people you would least suspect of having a political bone in their bodies. There was something in their psyche that drove them to be present. I can still see some contemporaries from my school days lining up and shuffling forward in quasi-military fashion to salute the dead hunger striker.

Rarely in my career had the role of the media come under such scrutiny. My work even impacted on my relationship with our Protestant neighbours in Belfast. Their attitude towards me changed and they started referring to me in conversation with Detta as 'he' or 'him' rather than 'Eamonn'. I lost my identity during those months. Every word a journalist uttered had to be measured and put on the scales. People were dying on the streets throughout this period, so the handling of information was a very delicate and sensitive matter. As journalists, we were under pressure to resist propaganda from all sides, but vested interests were pushing certain lines – not just within republicanism but also within the NIO. Besides this, we were listening to politicians, priests and clergy, who were meeting and sharing views with us in the wake of prison visits. There were days when I ended up getting just a few hours' sleep.

Among those who came to Northern Ireland to intervene, to try and persuade the hunger strikers to abandon their action, were members of the Red Cross. Practically every working journalist in Northern Ireland descended on the international airport to await their arrival. None of us had an idea what these people might look like, but I got a fixed idea in my head that they would be of Swiss or Austrian extraction, with blond hair, blue eyes, and wearing camel-coloured coats. Standing at the front of the pack, my microphone at the ready, I spotted two men whom I thought must be the Red Cross representatives. I thrust my microphone into their faces and asked, 'Gentlemen, what do you think you can bring to this situation at the Maze Prison?' One of the men looked at me and replied, 'You've got the wrong man – I come from Bangor.' My colleagues by now had pulled back and were quietly chuckling to themselves as I retreated with my tail between my legs. There were moments like that: moments when humour broke through, despite the gloom and the darkness of the day.

***

David Gilliland, who would go on to be one of the most senior and longest-serving civil servants in the NIO, was a member of the Stormont committee that monitored the hunger strike and advised what strategy should be adopted on behalf of the Thatcher government in London. While he was director of communications for the NIO, my relationship with him was uneven. It was he who used to tell new secretaries of state, 'Watch out for Mallie.' I was adjudged the wild child of broadcast journalism, known for not taking prisoners once my microphone was live.

Years later, I asked Gilliland if he would meet me to discuss his involvement in hunger-strike policy in 1981. When we met, he asked me, 'Did you think I'd meet you?' I told him I hadn't been sure. He replied, 'I'll tell you why: I always thought you were a wee cunt, but I knew one thing – you were only ever interested in the story.'

Gilliland's hunger-strike committee had an open line to the Cabinet Office, but Stormont and Downing Street didn't always see eye to eye on government policy around these issues. Gilliland said, 'London was shit-scared. They felt that we were giving the wrong advice. They were looking to the Foreign Office; the Foreign Office was not keen to give rise to trouble, fearing international criticism, but didn't care if forty died.' Another insider once told me that Thatcher hated nothing more than international criticism and had reacted very badly to the messages of disapproval of her IRA hunger-strike policy that were pouring in from embassies around the world.

Gilliland was unambiguous about where he and his committee stood on the fate of the hunger strikers. 'We felt that the hunger strike was a bid to get control of the prisons. The five demands would mean the Provos would run the prison. Once we conceded that, you couldn't tell the consequences ... They would determine who, what, et cetera and then the concept of prison was gone.'

Gilliland also drew attention to the propaganda skills of the republicans. 'They [Sinn Féin] were better than we were when it came to publicity. They were learning all the time. They published leaflets and photos to demonstrate what was going on. When we went to America, I remember seeing their leaflets on the desks of senators and congressmen on Capitol Hill. The leaflet was called "The Facts" and it contained glowing tributes to the hunger strikers: good fathers and good citizens. I said to myself, bully for you, Danny.' That was a reference to the propaganda skills of Danny Morrison, the director of publicity for Sinn Féin throughout that period.

What Gilliland was about to tell me shocked me, given the bluntness and directness of his exposition. He said, 'If we hadn't let them die, what would have been the consequences? Today the prisoners would be dictating what happens in the prisons. Once Maggie Thatcher saw the uproar, maybe she had a doubt, but on the central point of the principle she wouldn't have weakened. It was a tremendous gamble. It is one of the most courageous things the government ever did here. British governments were always shackled by their past, particularly the history of hunger strikes in Ireland. Once you decide a hunger strike is not going to be a weapon, it is no longer a weapon.'

Gilliland also explained the thinking behind the standard hunger-strike death announcement – only the name, date and time ever changed. 'I drafted the one statement regarding the death of the hunger strikers and that was a statement that became the formula because it was full of sympathy and concern – simple, suicide in prison. We had to treat this as if it was a perfectly routine prison issue – that a prisoner had committed suicide. Bobby Sands had all the facilities of the prison available to him, food and so on, but under the Tokyo Declaration he could not be force-fed.'

Gilliland also discussed the run-up to Sands' death. 'There was an occasion before Bobby Sands died in the early hours of the morning when there was a definite weakening in London. We were keeping London informed constantly on an open line. The Foreign Office/Cabinet Committee were saying, it seemed to us, "The game is not worth the candle."'

That was not how Gilliland and his colleagues viewed the situation. He told me, 'We were determined – the game was worth the candle. We were of the opinion that if we failed, we had sold the Prison Service down the river and the Provos would control the prisons ever more. We decided in Belfast that if the government weakened, we might call it a resignation matter. We, in the Belfast group, had decided that we could not allow the policy which we had followed consistently to be wiped out; to be told that we would have to compromise in some way. We felt we would have to go. The Cabinet had other issues to deal with and here were these bog Irishmen trying to kill themselves. We offered advice. They took the political decision.'

Gilliland's interpretation of the Cabinet Office's thinking on Sands was 'Let the hoor die.' He added, 'There is no doubt in my mind that it was the right decision.' Gilliland's approach, in terms of how the NIO committee addressed the hunger strike, was to make sure – in his parlance – that 'the pike went back in the thatch forever'. What Gilliland was saying, in essence, was that they were committed to making sure that the prisoners were defeated, in the hope that republicans wouldn't dare attempt in the future to take control of jails using hunger striking as a weapon. Only time will show if he was right. As with Terence MacSwiney, who lives on in folk memory in San Sebastián and all over the world, I suspect that Bobby Sands' name will resonate with generations yet unborn.

However, Sands is remembered by others, Margaret Thatcher made her feelings on the hunger strikers clear. In confidential State papers, she wrote, 'The people who had been killed by the Provisional IRA had had no choice. The hunger strikers had a choice.' On 28 May 1981, speaking at Stormont, she said of the IRA, 'Faced with the failure of their discredited cause, the men of violence have chosen in recent months to play what may well be their last card. They have turned their violence against themselves through the prison hunger strike to death. They seek to work on the most basic of human emotions – pity – as a means of creating tension and stoking the fires of bitterness and hatred.'

However, she appeared more sympathetic in personal papers unearthed by her official biographer, Charles Moore, saying, 'You have to hand it to some of these IRA boys,' and describing them as 'poor devils' because 'if they didn't go on strike they'd be shot [by their own side] ... What a waste! What a terrible waste of human life!'

Yet, according to Moore, the 'Iron Lady had been disingenuous over the Maze crisis in 1980'. Moore, who was given full access to the former prime minister's personal papers and government files, said Thatcher actually gave the go-ahead for secret talks with republicans during the hunger strikes. He contends that a high-ranking security officer had activated links to the IRA leadership through Derry businessman Brendan Duddy, who told him that Gerry Adams and Martin McGuinness 'wanted the hunger strike stopped'. Moore concludes, 'There can be no doubt, therefore, that Mrs Thatcher went against her public protestations about not negotiating with terrorists, and actively did so, though at a remove. The lady behind the veil had weakened.' But he explains, 'In [her] view this was a very different thing from direct talks between herself and other Ministers and Sinn Féin–IRA.'

In an interesting analysis on how the strikes affected her personally, Thatcher wrote in her memoirs, *The Downing Street Years*, 'Bobby Sands died on Tuesday 5 May. The date was of some significance for me personally, though I did not know it at the time. From this time forward I became the IRA's top target for assassination.' The IRA's 1984 Brighton bomb attack on the hotel in which she and her husband, Denis, were staying during her party conference, confirmed this.

***

The IRA was determined to make Margaret Thatcher pay for the death of Bobby Sands and the nine other prisoners. They knew months in advance that the Conservative Party's annual conference of 1984 would be taking place in Brighton. An IRA source told me, 'We realised we could actually get to her.'

In the early hours of the morning of 12 October 1984, the IRA struck at the heart of the British establishment when a bomb ripped through Brighton's Grand Hotel. Miraculously, the prime minister emerged physically unscathed, though the blast badly damaged her bathroom. Five people were killed and thirty-one were injured in the attack. As I lay in bed early that morning and heard the breaking news, I said a prayer of thanksgiving that Thatcher had survived the bombing. I was certain that had she been killed it would have led to an escalation of violence in Northern Ireland and people would have died as a result.

The IRA's statement of responsibility for the Brighton bombing was chilling: 'Mrs Thatcher will now realise that Britain cannot occupy our country and torture our prisoners and shoot our people in their own streets and get away with it. Today we were unlucky, but remember we only have to be lucky once. You will have to be lucky always. Give Ireland peace and there will be no war.'

In those days, a delightful woman helped us in our home a few days each week. She was with us for years before having to pull back through age. We loved her and she was an adopted granny to our children. She was better than any security guard, intelligent and ever vigilant. She had lived the greater part of her life among an entirely Protestant community in Kilburn Street off the Donegall Road in South Belfast. She was born into that tradition and married into it. She was a wonderful barometer for me against which to measure opinion and mood in the Protestant, loyalist, unionist communities. I was very interested to hear from Mrs Doak how people in her immediate community reacted to the IRA's attempt to kill Thatcher in Brighton. 'I heard people saying it was a pity they didn't get the aul bitch. That's God's truth,' she said. I can only conclude that a deep anger about the poll tax, the miners' strike and – perhaps especially – Thatcher's 1981 acknowledgement and acceptance that the Irish government had a legitimate right to be consulted on the affairs of Northern Ireland had left her with fewer friends than she'd once had in the side streets of the Donegall Road in South Belfast.

✳ ✳ ✳

Every doctor takes the Hippocratic oath, vowing ethically – among other things – to care for the sick and alleviate suffering above all else. Yet in 1981, in the Maze Prison, doctors had to watch their patients die before their eyes, and they were not allowed to feed them. The secrecy surrounding every aspect of the hunger strikes prompted me to dig more deeply into that era, and I had the opportunity on more than one occasion to speak with one of the doctors who had actually cared for some of the prisoners at their lowest point.

The senior doctor at the Maze Prison hospital during the hunger strikes was David Ross, a Presbyterian and former GP from Ballyclare. My source told me that he came at his work with a 'messianic fervour'. He had been in charge from the time of the first hunger strike in 1980, during which he treated South Armagh man Sean McKenna, the first republican to go on hunger strike. McKenna was virtually blind when Brendan Hughes, the IRA's officer commanding in the jail, believing concessions were on the way, gave clearance for him to come off his strike. Dr Ross claimed that the prisoners were duped at the end of the first hunger strike and he gave a strong indication that he was there when the deal was unveiled to the prisoners.

Ross was still the senior medical officer when the second strike began. My source told me, 'We were told David was finding it very difficult to deal with the situation. He became emotionally involved in the decline of the prisoners. He examined them every day but could not intervene. Perhaps he had an ethics problem. He had great difficulty, it appeared, coping with that, as had the nursing staff as the hunger strikers got more seriously ill. The real problem was at the point when the prisoners needed intensive nursing to avoid bedsores. They had to be turned over very often and laid on fleece or actual lambswool. People got very close to them.' At this stage Dr Ross was virtually living in the prison himself.

I was fascinated to hear from someone at the coalface what it was like to care for people who were choosing to starve themselves to death. My source continued, 'Three or four of us were drafted in to assist. My part was very small. I came along as two prisoners were dying. I examined them each day. We were meant to predict their deaths, so that the security forces could be alerted for the impact on the streets. Very little was told to me because we were quite new to the game.

'I thought they [the hunger strikers] sustained themselves through a spiritual element, an Easter element of martyrdom. Sometimes you have to think about the motivation of the IRA. It would be difficult to commit yourself to slow ritual suicide for a political ideal unless you had a strong spiritual or a religious motive behind it. The IRA were able to atone for something of the sins of the past because clearly through dying, that past could be put behind them.'

It was fascinating to listen to the very unexpected alternative perspective of a Protestant doctor treating members of the IRA, especially set against the tsunami of unionist derision and contempt for the hunger strikers.

In an interesting overview of the possible wellspring sustaining the commitment of hunger strikers who were prepared to die for their cause, the doctor concluded, 'Most suicides are associated with depression. These men were in good spirits and appeared mentally stable. They may have been deliberately isolated from each other so that they didn't know one had died. They were kept in individual rooms,' he said.

'You had ones who were up walking about, able to take exercise; ones who were able to sit up in bed, able to listen to the radio, fully compos mentis but needed a wheelchair to get out into the yard. Then you had ones being nursed on sheepskin, quite ill, gasping, in and out of consciousness. My interest was really in the ones who were very low. They looked like someone who was very old, pale, sunken cheeks, long hair, much older than their years, and their death appeared to be relatively painless to the onlooker, in that it began with this drifting in and out of consciousness, then became unconscious and then into a coma. That period from drifting in and out of consciousness to death might have taken two or three days.'

The granular detail of the doctor's account of watching somebody expiring while helplessly standing by unable to do anything to try to retrieve the situation was shocking. Despite these doctors' professional experience, the circumstances in which they now found themselves were something for which they could not ever have been prepared.

On 13 June 1986, Dr Ross returned to his Templepatrick home from the Maze. At around 6.20 p.m. he went to the garage next to his bungalow and attempted to take his life. His wife, Gladys, found him. He died four hours later at the Royal Victoria Hospital. An inquest found that Ross suffered from 'recurrent depressive illness' and was taking anti-depressants and anti-anxiety medication prescribed by his own doctor and a psychiatrist. Belfast coroner James Elliott concluded that the doctor's wounds were 'consistent with self-infliction'. My source added, 'I think Dr Ross felt his work hadn't been properly recognised.'

***

The IRA hunger strikes, the killing of Earl Mountbatten at Mullaghmore and the deaths of eighteen British soldiers in the double Narrow Water Castle bombing the same day, and the many other atrocities across Northern Ireland, meant British Prime Minister Margaret Thatcher frequented Northern Ireland more often than any other prime minister. During her tenure of office, I crossed her path during practically every visit she made here. My exchanges with her were always of a fractious nature, culminating in a remarkable development in December 1983, when she approved a recommendation by her chief press secretary, Bernard Ingham, to muzzle me as a correspondent. Ingham, now deceased, was a permanent fixture at Mrs Thatcher's side no matter where she went while she was prime minister. Declassified files contain a personal note in Ingham's handwriting to his boss singling me out for attention from all other working journalists in Northern Ireland.

Journalism is a rough trade, and the establishment is a considerable force if it turns its guns on anyone rattling its cage. As a political correspondent, I was automatically acquainted with all prime ministerial visits to Northern Ireland. I always found Mrs Thatcher to be of a bossy disposition, brusque, avoiding small talk, her mind set on saying what she had pre-arranged to say with few opportunities for a sit-down interview or for a one-on-one interview.

I had access to Thatcher in the wake of Sinn Féin's electoral success in 1983 on the two parts of the island of Ireland. Emboldened by their first venture into constitutional politics with Sands and building on the upsurge in backing for the hunger strikers, the leadership of Sinn Féin had decided to contest the general election in June 1983 in the Irish Republic.

Two IRA prisoners were elected, Kieran Doherty in Cavan-Monaghan and Paddy Agnew in Louth. Also elected that year were Alex Maskey, as a councillor in Belfast City Hall, and Gerry Adams, who was elected MP for West Belfast, although he abstained from attending Westminster.

Clearly, however, my style of interviewing politicians was coming under scrutiny in Downing Street. When I sat down in front of the prime minister in Parliament Buildings during one of her regular visits to Northern Ireland, I touched a raw nerve when I reminded her of her 1981 claim that 'the men of violence have chosen in recent months to play what may well be their last card'. I was in her face, challenging, 'Do you still believe that?' The interview came to an abrupt end. As I left the room, you could have cut the atmosphere with a knife. I was scarcely out the door when a furious Mrs Thatcher declared in front of all present, including the Press Association's correspondent Deric Henderson, 'What a horrible man!'

As a result, Bernard Ingham set about making sure what had passed between his boss and me would not be repeated. This was his recommendation to Mrs Thatcher:

10 Downing Street
Agreed MT
Prime Minister.

Northern Ireland Media:

I would like a clear steer from you for future planning on the handling of the media during any visit. You have agreed to speak before the camera, rather as you did in Stormont on the last occasion, instead of holding a press conference. In fact you have not given a press conference in Northern Ireland, but you have allowed yourself to be doorstepped and to be interviewed by radio and television.

The effect of this has been to give maximum offence to the writing press and to provide a platform for some pretty suspect people like Malley [*sic*] of Downtown Radio, who gets close to choking you with his microphone.

I would be much happier if you confined the visit to:

- camera shots: after all your objective is to be seen there;
- no doorstep or radio and TV interviews;
- a straight to camera statement at the end of the visit.

Ingham 13/12.

Yes
MT

For Ingham to suggest in writing that I was 'suspect' was not just nasty but potentially libellous. That said, I hope he is resting in peace. As for the Iron Lady, she was not for turning and neither was I. *Go gcumhdaí Dia thú*, Mrs Thatcher.

On 16 November 1990, Thatcher flew into Northern Ireland on what was to be her last visit there. The sword of Damocles was hanging over her in the form of a leadership challenge from her former defence secretary, Michael Heseltine (nicknamed Tarzan). Security was at a peak as Mrs Thatcher's Wessex helicopter took off from Aldergrove into the driving rain and wind, Fermanagh bound, flying low over Lough Neagh, and the rolling hills of Tyrone and the Fermanagh lakes. The security chiefs knew only too well that the IRA was in possession of Libyan ground-to-air missiles and the flight path was close to Clogher, only a few miles from the border with the Irish Republic, where army helicopters had been fired on several times.

According to the Press Association journalist on board the helicopter, at times, particularly over the villages of Augher and Fivemiletown, the helicopter was barely 100 feet above the treetops, a flying technique designed to thwart machine-gun or missile attack. Indeed, Thatcher's helicopter flew so low that her private secretary Charles Powell joked, 'It was the first time we have flown underground.' Her press secretary Bernard Ingham added, 'We even heard the cattle ducking.'

Thatcher's first port of call was Leaf Electronics outside Enniskillen. As she moved around the room engaging members of staff, I formulated a non-provocative question in my head as the media was obsessing with her imminent departure.

'Are you here to say "good bye" to some old friends?' I asked. (I overheard Bob Templeton, the deputy director of communications in the NIO saying, 'That's a googly if I ever saw one'.) 'Certainly not,' snapped Mrs Thatcher. 'This visit has been planned for some time.' When she was reminded that a MORI poll had put Heseltine ahead of her as a better bet to lead the Tories to a fourth term, she was defiant, declaring, 'I believe we shall win and win well.'

Ten days later came Thatcher's last day in office. That was a Wednesday. In her memoir she described how the tears began just after 9 a.m. when she said goodbye to No. 10 staff before her final audience with the Queen.

'Some were in tears,' she wrote. 'I tried to hold back mine, but they flowed freely as I walked down the hall past those applauding me on my way out of office ...'

Before going outside, she paused to collect her thoughts with her loyal aide and confidante Cynthia Crawford. More tears. 'Crawfie wiped a trace of mascara off my cheek, evidence of a tear which I had been unable to check,' Lady Thatcher wrote.

She went outside and, again tearfully, said, 'We're leaving Downing Street for the last time after eleven-and-a-half wonderful years and we're happy to leave the UK in a very much better state than when we came here.'

Chapter Five

Gibraltar

THE BULK OF THE IRA's violent campaign was concentrated in Northern Ireland, but at different points its ruling body, the Army Council, chose to broaden its theatre of operations. This led to attacks not just in Britain but anywhere the British government had a presence. In July 1976, the British ambassador in Dublin, Christopher Ewart-Biggs, was blown up by a 200lb bomb near his official residence. Richard Sykes, British ambassador to the Netherlands, was shot dead by the IRA in The Hague in March 1979. Various British Army bases in Europe, for example in Germany, were also targeted by IRA teams.

On Sunday 6 March 1988, Detta, the children and I were having our evening meal at home when news started coming through of a shooting in Gibraltar, a British Overseas Territory, involving people from Ireland. For the rest of the evening, I listened to every radio bulletin and watched every television news programme. It transpired that the IRA had dispatched a hit-team consisting of five members, three men and two women. The IRA squad included Danny McCann, Mairéad Farrell and Seán Savage. They had made their way from Belfast to Spain with the intention of planting a bomb to target an army band scheduled to play in Gibraltar town centre. However, British Intelligence was ahead of the IRA, and the British Army's Special Air Service (SAS) ambushed the republican unit – unarmed at that moment – shooting three of them dead in what was called 'Operation Flavius' (Flavius Aetius was a Roman general in the closing period of the Western Roman Empire).

How the SAS found out about the IRA's planned operation is still a mystery. According to one senior member of the Royal Ulster Constabulary (RUC), the police realised that well-known individuals had left the Northern Ireland jurisdiction. There was also a report that intelligence about the planned mission had been picked up by the security services in a Belfast city-centre bar, but I have failed to substantiate that. What I do know is that Danny McCann had prepared for every outcome and had left behind an 'If I don't return' letter for his family and friends.

Those killings in Gibraltar would turn Northern Ireland inside out in the coming weeks, to the point that it felt as if we were living on the edge of civil war. Even the repatriation of the bodies of the IRA trio sparked serious tension between the police and republicans. All sorts of allegations were levelled at the authorities to do with the way in which they were perceived to be interfering in the arrangements for the return of the bodies to the victims' families.

On 16 March, several thousand mourners turned out for the funerals of the 'Gibraltar Three' in Milltown Cemetery in West Belfast. I didn't see any police or army on the ground while the funerals were taking place and that seemed odd to me. These funerals were otherwise like all previous republican funerals I had covered in West Belfast, except for one other fact: this time, three members of the IRA were being interred at the same time, buried side by side.

However, as so often happened during the Troubles, nothing was as it seemed. As the coffin of Seán Savage was being lowered into a grave in the republican plot, I was leaning against the iron railings holding up my microphone to record everything that was being said and what was happening. Suddenly there was a thud behind me. Debris and a puff of black smoke filled the air. A grenade had bounced off a headstone about ten feet away from me. A bearded man wearing a cap and carrying a gun continued hurling grenades as he ran through the cemetery. Mourners were, by then, chasing him as he headed for the motorway through a long stretch of boggy waste ground. As all this was happening, I kept asking myself two questions: 'Is there a bomb in the grave?' and 'Is my tape recorder definitely capturing all this?' Fortunately, there was no bomb in the grave and my tape recorder was working.

Meanwhile, while his fellow republicans had hit the deck, Gerry Adams was standing tall, like a general commanding his troops, on the elevated ground beside the graves. He kept calling out, 'Come back, come back, young people,' but many of them continued charging after the gunman, who every so often wheeled around, took aim and shot at them. There was pandemonium; it was like a scene from a violent film.

I caught something else happening out of the corner of my eye at that point – a young man was being targeted by members of the crowd. It turned out that *Belfast Telegraph* reporter Noel Doran, now editor of *The Irish News*, had been attempting to leave the graveyard to find a landline to file copy to his news desk. As he neared the fence that bordered Milltown Cemetery and Eastwood's scrapyard, Doran told me he was intercepted and challenged about where he was going. He was then approached by a number of men who grabbed him and started thumping him. He recognised one of those hitting him – Cleeky Clarke, a well-known republican, who was stewarding the funerals. In desperation, Doran shouted, 'You know me, Cleeky. I am a journalist.' Clarke took control immediately and stopped the assault. By this stage Danny Morrison, Sinn Féin's director of communications, had arrived, and he made sure Doran was okay. I can only conclude some of the crowd reacted spontaneously on spotting a figure unknown to them hurrying away in the midst of the gun-and-grenade assault on the funeral, perhaps suspecting he was a second gunman.

. When the crowd caught up with the actual gunman, he was beaten unconscious and might well have been killed had the police not arrived. We would later learn that the attacker was a member of the UDA, Michael Stone, who operated alone a lot of the time. It was suggested in media circles that he had been among the congregation during one of the IRA funeral Masses, and had slipped out to the cemetery ahead of the departure of the cortège. Stone appeared out of nowhere in the cemetery – he is thought to have been hiding behind a headstone – waiting for the appropriate moment to strike.

I had just lived through a very scary few minutes, far too close to grenades and bullets, but three men died as a result of the grenade-and-gun attack: Thomas McErlean, John Murray and a young man called Kevin Brady. Sixty-six people were hurt. What had started in Gibraltar when the SAS had killed the IRA trio had triggered this spiral of vicious violence across Northern Ireland.

On 19 March, another large crowd was making its way to Milltown Cemetery to attend the funeral of Kevin Brady. As his cortège processed down the Andersonstown Road, a Volkswagen Passat drove towards it, stopped, reversed and ended up hemmed in by some of the black taxis accompanying the funeral. In the wake of Stone's attack three days earlier, the mourners were on edge and assumed the occupants of the car were loyalists. As it turned out, they were two army corporals who, inexplicably, had driven into the cortège. The crowd set upon the car immediately and one of the corporals fired a warning shot, but it failed to drive back the frenetic crowd. I wasn't covering that funeral, but even watching the denouement on television was a shocking spectacle. The angry crowd rushed towards the car – people climbed onto its roof, smashed the windows with an iron bar and hauled the two men from the vehicle during a desperate struggle.

An IRA source later told me, 'After the Michael Stone attack three days earlier, it was decided that several people would "carry" [weapons] on the periphery of Brady's funeral. Four or five were armed, with another IRA team floating about with access to an arms dump nearby. We came to the gate of Casement Park and one volunteer handed us the soldiers' identity cards. We established they were SAS. [In fact, the soldiers were Signals engineers.] We commandeered a black taxi. We brought the black taxi round to the wall, where the soldiers were lying. There were two people in the taxi. The remaining members of the squad jumped into a car and followed the taxi. The soldiers were taken out of the taxi and shot with their own gun. To the squad of men, it was a good hit. They were SAS to all intents and purposes. The fact that Dan McCann and Mairéad Farrell were colleagues meant we felt we were getting something back for the Gibraltar shootings.'

Father Alec Reid, a priest based at Clonard Monastery in West Belfast, told me that as the soldiers were being dragged into Casement Park, 'at one stage, one of them was holding my hand like a child holding his father's hand. I felt that he felt secure at that time but quickly a "military operation" took over and I no longer had any control.' The soldiers were stripped and beaten, before being taken to waste ground and shot. Father Reid told me that he had made his way to the waste ground. He was captured on camera pressing his mouth to that of one of the soldiers, trying to resuscitate him. When he straightened up, his lips had the soldier's blood on them. Journalist Mary Holland, who witnessed the scene, wrote, 'His courage and compassion redeemed us all. It sent one image of Ireland across the world that spoke of human pity in the face of death, rather than the savagery of the mob.' No act could have done more to show the world for what Father Reid stood.

A lethal chain of events, which started in Gibraltar on 6 March, had ended thirteen days later in Belfast, with a total of eight dead and sixty-eight hurt. Margaret Thatcher described the deaths of the soldiers as 'an act of appalling savagery'. The sight of young British soldiers being ferociously attacked in view of the world's press and television cameras left a huge mark on the British psyche in a way that earlier deaths had not. However, the most enduring image from that time remains that of Father Reid kneeling over one of the soldier's practically naked body prostrate on the ground, administering the last rites.

Over the years Father Reid pursued a mission to end all violence, but he was fully aware that he was working in a community that was an IRA heartland, and he accepted that he couldn't treat the perpetrators of the violence like lepers if he were to be successful in his mission. He and fellow priest Father Gerry Reynolds dedicated their lives to the search for peace, fortunately living long enough to see the fruits of their labour. They kept the faith.

***

An inquest into the deaths of the three IRA members was scheduled in Gibraltar for 6 September 1988. This hearing would decide if the killings had been lawful. A considerable debate about whether to send someone to cover the inquest raged in the newsroom at Downtown Radio. I held the view that, as the local radio station with a reputation for being first with the news, we should be there. In contrast, my head of news, David Sloan, wasn't confident that there would be sufficient local interest in this particular event, but he was overruled by Chief Executive Ivan Tinman. I was dispatched to Gibraltar and flew out the next day, leaving my wife home alone with our young children and no family support whatsoever. On reflection it was unfair and selfish of me.

I had no love for Gibraltar or empathy with its people when we were there. In 1981, Detta and I had visited there when were on holiday in the south of Spain and I felt the place lacked a soul. It had that feeling of being halfway to nowhere, with Spain standing on its toes and its homeland – the UK – seeming as distant from it as the man on the moon.

During the Gibraltar inquest, high-profile Belfast solicitor Patrick McGrory represented the families of the IRA members.

His wife, Phyllis, accompanied her husband to Gibraltar and was by his side at all times when he wasn't in court. John Laws QC represented the British government, Michael Hucker acted for the Ministry of Defence and Feliz Pizzarello was the coroner. The various soldiers giving evidence were behind screens and named only as Soldier A, B, C, etc. It was the most extraordinary inquest.

Initially there was contempt for McGrory in the British press because he was acting on behalf of the families of the IRA dead, but it seemed to me their attitudes towards him mellowed as a result of the strength of his advocacy and his learnedness. The contest between McGrory and his English counterparts was hot and heavy at times. As the English legal duo sought to counter McGrory's line of argument that as unarmed combatants they were illegally killed, they reminded me of two slices of toast popping up in a toaster at the same time, occasionally colliding in their desperate efforts to rob their counterpart of any potential advantage. McGrory was one of the most literary and cultured individuals imaginable, and was very familiar with Spain, having spent a lot of time there in the 1950s when Franco was still in power. During his exposition on behalf of the families of Mairéad Farrell, Danny McCann and Seán Savage, he drew on Spanish literature to underscore the manner in which the SAS had cut down the three IRA members, referencing Spanish poet García Lorca, who captured the very essence of the death of the bull in the bullring in his poem 'A las cinco de la tarde' (At five in the afternoon). As a Spanish graduate, it was very special for me to witness how Spain's culture seeped into the proceedings.

I remained in Gibraltar for two weeks covering the inquest, reporting daily and hourly on every twist and turn. It had triggered great interest not just in Northern Ireland but also in Great Britain. The absence of a security presence in and around the coroners' court came as something of a surprise to us journalists from Belfast – we were normally tripping over RUC members at the Crumlin Road courthouse during republican and loyalist trials.

Most of the journalists reporting on the inquest were staying at the Holiday Inn, not far from the court. During the inquest I fell quite ill, so ill that even the reception staff at the hotel realised that I was in a bad way. They sent for a doctor, who casually asked me from where I came. I said that I lived in Belfast, and he set about asking me about people he knew in Ireland. He then informed me that he had studied medicine at Trinity College. I started to get better very quickly. He also told me that he'd married an O'Malley from Limerick, which explained why he was so conversant with so many aspects of life on the island of Ireland. What a coincidence.

I recovered and returned home, realising that the inquest was going to last for longer than we had anticipated. Downtown's head of news remained unsure about the story and didn't think I should go back for the last week, but Tinman once again argued that I should be there, so I returned to Gibraltar. The jury found that the authorities had acted lawfully in killing the IRA personnel. That was no surprise given that they were all local to a place where the IRA had been planning to plant a bomb. On the final day of the inquest, in a strange coincidence, the Red Arrows flew over Gibraltar. Some members of the British press stood and saluted as the planes roared across the sky.

That Gibraltar inquest was a unique experience in my career. A remarkable camaraderie developed among many of the journalists based in Gibraltar for the inquest, and we retired nightly for supper to a restaurant in Spain. We frequented a bistro in the hills where it was not uncommon for a pig to be on the spit. As a student of Spanish, I acted as interpreter for my fellow journalists.

When I returned home, I discovered just how much the inquest had impacted upon the consciousness of the people. One of the soldiers about whom we had reported over and over again was Soldier F, who had been in charge of Operation Flavius on the ground in Gibraltar. The ongoing mention of Soldier F in the news sparked a lot of comment back home. Proof of this surfaced in an unusual set of circumstances. During the inquest, Northern Ireland was playing the Republic of Ireland at Windsor Park, and Northern Ireland was not doing particularly well. This prompted a wit in the Kop stand to shout at Billy Bingham, the team manager, 'For fuck's sake, Billy, bring on soldier F.' The stadium erupted I am told.

✳✳✳

At the time of the Gibraltar killings, Patrick Mayhew was the attorney general in Britain. In 1992, he was appointed secretary of state for Northern Ireland. Very early in his tenure, he asked his staff to set up a meeting with the solicitor Patrick McGrory. McGrory's son Barra told me that his father was curious and accepted the invitation. In the course of the meeting, Mayhew said one of the reasons he wanted to meet McGrory personally was to pass on 'good wishes' from John Laws, the barrister who had represented the British government at the Gibraltar inquest. Mayhew told McGrory that Laws, who was now an appeal-court judge, had been impressed with his advocacy skills.

That wasn't the only reason for the meeting, however. Mayhew was on another mission and had clearly done his homework on McGrory. The Belfast solicitor had been Gerry Adams' legal advisor for decades. He had been responsible for negotiating Adams' release from the Maze in 1972 so that he could attend the talks at Cheyne Walk between republicans and William Whitelaw, then the UK secretary of state for Northern Ireland. McGrory was live to the real reason for the meeting when Mayhew asked him if he thought that – in the event of a peace deal – Adams could bring the IRA membership with him. Mayhew was using McGrory as a sounding board to determine whether Adams could deliver a ceasefire in the right circumstances. Unknown to the outside world, Mayhew was laying the foundations for history yet unborn.

In 2020, Dominic Cummings, Prime Minister Boris Johnson's most influential and controversial advisor, hit the headlines for breaking the Covid-19 lockdown rules – some of which he wrote – driving 264 miles to Durham with his wife and young son. I'm always interested in finding out about people's backgrounds: where they were educated and why they landed where they landed in life. I wasn't disappointed in the case of Cummings. I discovered that his uncle was none other than John Laws. At the same time as Cummings was travelling to Durham and staying there in a house adjacent to his family home, his mother's brother, his favourite uncle, Laws, was seriously ill with coronavirus. He died within two weeks of the Cummings controversy breaking. Covid restrictions meant that Cummings could not attend the funeral. What fascinated me about all of this was how the paths of these people crossed in one way or another – McGrory, Mayhew, Laws and Cummings. There is, aptly, a Spanish expression to sum this up: '*El mundo es un pañuelo*' – the English equivalent goes like this: 'It's a small world.'

Chapter Six

Peace Comes Dropping Slow

ANY COMMENTARY ON THE Northern Ireland Peace Process ought to include the cold, hard fact that over 3,500 people lost their lives during the Troubles at the hands of the IRA, loyalists and the State. The end product – empty chairs, broken homes and broken hearts.

The date of 5 October 1968 in Derry is deemed to be the start of the Troubles in Northern Ireland. A march was proposed by activists on the Derry Housing Action Committee (DHAC), which had been founded in early 1968. That body was campaigning against discrimination in housing and the shortage of social housing in one of Northern Ireland's most depressed towns. During the protest, the RUC was caught on camera batoning certain people in Derry's Duke Street, images of which were flashed around the world. Gerry Fitt MP ended up with a split skull, blood running down his face. I was still at school back then, learning the meaning of civil rights, but I walked in the civil rights march in Newry on 11 January 1969. That was the first time I met Bernadette Devlin, who would end up being the face of the campaign for justice all over the world. I have interviewed the now Bernadette Devlin McAliskey several times down the years. She was to politics in the sixties and seventies, with her heightened awareness of political injustices, what Irish singer Sinéad O'Connor emerged as in the nineties, highlighting social injustices on the island of Ireland – particularly cases of child abuse by some clergy and how women were being treated in a male-dominated society. Both paid a heavy price for their humanity.

They were not the only ones – the Peace Process was hard won. While there were many bends in the road leading to peace, essentially there were three critical stages involving the following key figures: Cardinal Tomás Ó Fiaich; Father Alec Reid; former Sinn Féin President Gerry Adams; Vice President Martin McGuinness; former Taoiseach Charles J. Haughey; former SDLP leader John Hume; Prime Minister Tony Blair; Taoisigh Albert Reynolds and Bertie Ahern; Northern Ireland Secretaries of State Peter Brooke and Mo Mowlam; US President Bill Clinton; UUP leader David Trimble; David Ervine and Dawn Purvis of the Progressive Unionist Party (PUP); Gary McMichael of the Ulster Democratic Party; Monica McWilliams of the Women's Coalition; and Martha Pope, chief aide to Senator George Mitchell, who chaired the Good Friday negotiations. I single these individuals out because each one of them had a steady hand on the tiller at one time or another during the making of the Peace Process.

Dublin-born priest Father Reid lived in the republican heartland of West Belfast, as did fellow priest Father Des Wilson. They didn't take the moral high ground, demonising republicans wedded to the use of so-called 'armed struggle'.

They didn't choose, like so many other Catholic Church leaders, to turn their backs on their own people. Reid literally spilled his sweat, coming close to spilling his blood, trying to replace violence with an alternative addressing what were judged by republicans to be injustices, not just socially and economically but constitutionally as well. He was forced to step back from community work in the wake of the 1981 hunger-strike deaths in the Maze Prison. He was burnt-out due to the stress of the strike and the loss of life in jail and on the streets. He had also been involved in efforts to stop inter-republican feuding in the seventies. It was back then that he got to know Gerry Adams, recently released from prison. The coincidence of Adams' cousin Kevin Hannaway living close to Clonard Monastery, home to Father Reid, helped to cement the relationship and interaction between Adams and the priest over the years.

From the early eighties, the 'silent' priest, affectionately known in republican circles as 'the Sagart' (the Irish for priest), was tirelessly knocking on doors and writing letters and papers to build a framework within which to help end all violence. Another fellow human rights priest and activist, Father Raymond Murray, shared his thoughts with me about Reid: 'His motive was a humanitarian one – bluntly, to stop the killing. He came to Armagh to see me in a mood of great anxiety. He said to me a number of times: "When you are faced with this problem you must face it in a realistic way. How do you get the republicans to stop the war – what would tip the balance to get the IRA to stop?"' Murray added, 'His main plan was to help Sinn Féin to gain complete control over the republican movement, and then to build an alliance of nationalist parties, respecting party differences but all working for peace.'

Gerry Adams outlined to me the challenge for republicans which he faced in pursuing a strictly peaceful path: 'The Irish and British governments – from Sunningdale in December 1973 through to the Anglo-Irish Agreement in 1985 and the Downing Street Declaration in 1993 – were about defending and protecting the status quo. They were about stabilising and pacifying rather than about removing the injustice that was driving political dissent and resistance. The policies of both governments sought to criminalise and marginalise republicans.' He continued, 'Peace building requires a different approach. Peace is not simply about ending conflict. It has to tackle the causes of conflict. Peace must therefore mean justice'.

The interaction between Father Reid, Father Murray and Adams resulted in an agreement that Reid would make an approach to former Taoiseach Charles Haughey, then in opposition in the Republic of Ireland. The former Sinn Féin president had come to realise that without the involvement of the Irish government, there could be no political solution to the Troubles in Northern Ireland. Adams wanted a face-to-face meeting with Haughey. In the eighties, the former Sinn Féin president had concluded that republicanism had to become more outward-looking and less hubristic, reaching out not just to Church leaders, trade unions and political parties but also to people like Ken Livingstone, the 'hard left' leader of Greater London Council, and to future Labour Party MP and leader Jeremy Corbyn. He was now also looking to new horizons, to the Irish-American diaspora, while tapping into the extraordinary winds of change blowing in South Africa. Father Murray told me, 'The emphasis was on trying to persuade Haughey to meet Adams and thus give the project real credibility.' Reid was to let Haughey know that, in the opinion of Adams, a face-to-face meeting would strengthen his hand in trying to wean the IRA off violence.

At this time, Reid was continually putting together position papers on common nationalist grounds that might meet with the approval of three sides – the Irish government, the SDLP and Sinn Féin. By then we were entering stage two of the emerging Peace Process, despite the fact that no one necessarily saw it in these terms back in 1986. Adams and Reid initially pinned their hopes very much on the SDLP's deputy leader, Seamus Mallon, in the wake of the 1985 publication of the Thatcher/FitzGerald Anglo-Irish Agreement. They felt Mallon was 'greener' than Hume and would line up with Haughey in opposition to the Anglo-Irish Agreement. According to Adams, Mallon backed out of several planned meetings with Sinn Féin.

Father Reid's next port of call was Abbeyville, Kinsealy, in North Dublin, to meet Haughey. In previous publications I have revealed some of the facts about Reid's exchanges with Haughey, but the former taoiseach did not confide in me any details of papers in his possession which reflected Gerry Adams' thinking back in 1986–7, accessed by him during meetings with Reid. However, my fellow journalist, Ed Moloney, managed to persuade Haughey to allow him access to Reid's correspondence, and he lays bare a fascinating early indication of the Sinn Féin leader's planned march down a strictly constitutional road. He writes, 'From 1985/6 onwards, courtesy of Father Reid, Gerry Adams was also sending written messages to Mr Haughey, exploring ideas. Nothing was put in writing until May 1987 when a letter was composed and delivered to Kinsealy, thus formally launching the peace process.' Moloney states that in

Adams' letter, he sets out terms for an IRA ceasefire in which it is possible to discern the principles – and compromises – that underlay what became the Belfast Agreement. Moloney further highlights the fact that the Adams–Haughey communication reveals that Adams was actively contemplating a ceasefire and a wholly political strategy at a time when the IRA leadership was committed to intensifying violence. It was hoped the letter, containing a statement of principles, would help to deliver peace and an end to all violence. The conclusion reached by Moloney is that the Sinn Féin leader had for many years been working to 'a pre-cooked agenda' not necessarily shared by all his colleagues. Chief aide to Gerry Adams, Richard McAuley, told me, 'When the Sagart was talking to Haughey it was Adams' voice in his head that was talking.'

In another communication to Haughey, Father Reid wrote:

These principles as I understand them may be set out as follows:

1. The aim of 'the armed struggle' is to establish the right of all the Irish people to decide their own political future through dialogue among themselves. The establishment of a 32-county socialist republic is not therefore the aim of this struggle. From the Sinn Féin point of view this is a political ideal to be pursued and achieved by political strategies only.

2. The British must in some formal and credible way declare their willingness to set aside the claim enshrined in the Government of Ireland Act, 1920 that they have in their own right the power of veto

of the democratic decisions of the Irish people as a whole. In practice it would be sufficient for them to declare their willingness to set aside the Government of Ireland Act, 1920 in view of any agreements that the representatives of the people of Ireland in dialogue among themselves might make about their constitutional and political future.

Such a declaration would set the scene for a ceasefire by the IRA.

This principle relates only to the right of veto which the British authorities claim in Ireland on the basis of the 1920 Act. It should not therefore be taken to mean that Sinn Féin want the British to withdraw from Ireland at the present time. On the contrary they accept and would even insist on the need for a continuing British presence to facilitate the processes through which the constitutional and political structures of a just and lasting peace would be firmly and properly laid by the democratic decisions of the Irish people as a whole.

Once the representatives of all the Irish people, nationalist and unionist, could meet together in accordance with the principle of independence outlined in (2) above, all options for a settlement of the national question, for organising the constitutional and political structures of a just and lasting peace would be open for dialogue and decision.

While Charles Haughey told me he was intrigued by what he had seen and heard, meeting Adams was a bridge too far.

He feared the consequences of a leak about any face-to-face meeting with Adams during the lead into a general election. The Fianna Fáil leader could not get away from the ghost of the Arms Trial of 1970, at the outset of the Troubles, when he was accused of being involved in attempts to import arms to Ireland for the IRA. He vigorously denied that he had any knowledge that monies were misappropriated to help arm Northern republicans and was acquitted on 23 October. Haughey pushed back against meeting Adams despite the best efforts of Father Reid, but he advised Reid, 'if SDLP leader John Hume agrees to meet Gerry Adams he will be my proxy'.

A new front in the pursuit of peace in these islands was opening up. Irish civil servant Bill Nolan later told me of a conversation he had with Father Reid, in which the Clonard priest revealed that he had climbed Sugarloaf Mountain in County Wicklow after meeting Haughey. Reid told Nolan, 'I wanted to be nearer to the Holy Ghost to get all the inspiration I could get to help me with the wording of my letter to John Hume.' Clearly the Belfast-based priest was following the biblical example of Moses, who fasted for forty days and forty nights on Mount Sinai before coming down with the Ten Commandments. Mark Durkan, a chief advisor to Hume, assured me that the SDLP leader showed him Reid's letter in spring 1987.

***

'Would you listen to yourself because I have to.' This was a frequent response from John Hume when someone misrepresented what he had said, or if someone was putting forward an argument that made no sense. He was one politician to whom I paid a lot of attention, right through my formative years. I was influenced by him on two fronts: his opposition to the use of violence for political ends and his belief in the importance of a united Europe to stop wars.

Hume's modus operandi as a politician was interesting. Knowing that he was dealing with difficult political concepts, such as referendums, the right to self-determination, the consent principle and so on, he sought to convince everyone – from republicans to senior civil servants in London, Dublin, Europe and the US – of the rightness of his approach to resolving Northern Ireland's apparently intractable problem. But he also wanted to make sure that members of the media understood his way of thinking so that they could accurately report and explain it. I was one of the journalists invited by him to come up to his holiday home in Donegal, where he would bring me into a room and show me a piece of paper on which he had outlined his latest political thinking. I was free to read and study it, but I was not at liberty to take it away.

In reality, what Hume was giving me during those visits was advance insight into future key lines of thinking so that, when he put his thinking into the public domain, people like me were in a strong position to analyse and to explain his political direction of travel. In addition, the phone could ring at any moment of the day and he would be at the end of the line to alert me about his latest thinking or, for example during the hunger strikes in 1981, to bring me up to date on the very latest happenings inside the prisons. There has been nobody in the last 100 years in these islands who has been as politically imaginative as Hume who was also armed with the appropriate language to give effect to his ideas. He was a consummate constitutionalist who dedicated his life to the search for peace.

Right from the outset, all my conversations with John Hume were in the most part strictly professional. We rarely discussed families, education, musical interests or holidays, for example. In other words, there was very little small talk. I didn't ever find Hume to be gregarious. At large gatherings, he regularly ambled about, appearing to be lost inside his own head. There was something of the monk about him throughout his life. That is not to say that the SDLP leader was in any way lacking in personality. Many times, in Washington, at party conferences and at other events, I heard him belting out a song with the best of them. On one occasion he talked to me about his childhood; how he would sit at one end of the table doing his homework while, at the other end, his father filled in forms for poor people in their neighbourhood in Derry. That was the young Hume's apprenticeship, how he learned the meaning of public service. In 1975, years later, the boy who shared a table with his community-minded father would take a piece of paper and sketch out his vision for a resolution to the political deadlock in Northern Ireland. Dr Maurice Hayes, renowned public servant, with whom Hume had been staying after addressing an SDLP meeting in Strangford in County Down, later described that paper as 'the blueprint for the Good Friday Agreement of 1998 – at its heart were three sets of relationships'.

I lost count of the number of times I listened to what was known as the SDLP leader's 'Single Transferable Speech', also referred to as 'Humespeak'. It varied in content but remained consistent in messaging. My ears were sore listening to phrases like 'three sets of relationships'; 'unity of hearts, not unity of territory'; 'spill sweat not blood'; and 'you can't eat a flag', to name just a few. One of his key tools was repetition. His daughter Mo once told me that she'd said to her father that if she heard him repeating one of his political mantras one more time, she would scream. Hume used to reply, 'For the brightest pupil in the class you have to say it at least twenty times to be absolutely certain it goes in.'

In one of my first major interviews with John Hume, he painted a picture of his earliest acquaintance with public service. He told me, 'I'll never forget my first political lesson when I was ten years old. The nationalist party was holding an election meeting at the top of the street and waving their flags and my father who was unemployed saw that I was getting emotional. He put his hand on my shoulder. He said, "Don't get involved in that stuff son."

'I said, "Why not Dad?" He says, "You can't eat a flag." Think of the wisdom of that – that real politics should not be about waving flags. It should be about developing the standard of living of all sections of your people and that is common ground because both sections need that. And now our people have started working together through their representatives spilling their sweat not their blood and I look forward.

'That is what I call the healing process. As they work together they break down the barriers of the past and a new society in Ireland North and South will evolve – but it will not give victory to either side, it will be based on agreement and respect for differences.'

John Hume was also a man with a rare instinct. He argued forcefully against SDLP colleagues taking part in an anti-internment march in Derry on 30 January 1972. That day would become known as Bloody Sunday – during the march, members of the Parachute Regiment opened fire and shot dead thirteen innocent civilians, injuring another so severely that he died four months later. Many others were seriously wounded. Hume had intuited that the Paras were out for blood – an instinct shaped by what he had witnessed and experienced eight days earlier on Magilligan Strand. During that anti-internment protest, the Paras had to be prevented by their senior officers from using excessive force to break up the march.

Paddy O'Hanlon, nationalist MP for South Armagh from 1969 to 1974, whom I knew well, did not conceal from me the disappointment he had felt that day when Hume refused to march on 30 January. Hume later described Bloody Sunday as, 'dreadful, the worst day in the history of this city in my lifetime.' His support for the families of the victims knew no bounds, and one of his greatest contributions to their campaign for justice was to persuade Tony Blair to set up an independent inquiry into the events of Bloody Sunday in 1998.

When the 1974 Northern Ireland power-sharing executive was torn down by Ian Paisley and loyalists, the Northern Ireland Constitutional Convention was put in place in an attempt to resurrect politics in Northern Ireland. In 1975 Lord Chief Justice Robert Lowry was appointed chair of this new body. He was watching cricket in his room when John Hume and an SDLP delegation arrived for a meeting. The judge instructed his tipstaff to turn off the cricket, adding, 'I am sure John would not have much interest in that.' In response, Hume said, 'Do you think not? I played cricket for both City of Derry and Waterside CC. Remember one thing. We were always good at playing you boys at your own game.' Hume was remembered as a decent slow left-arm bowler and middle-order bat.

He was also an innovator. By the late seventies, he had cemented a special relationship with four of the most influential politicians on Capitol Hill in the US, who were known as the Four Horsemen: Senator Edward Kennedy, Senator Daniel Moynihan, Tip O'Neill (former Speaker of the House of Representatives), and New York Governor Hugh Carey. He realised that to achieve political change locally it was necessary to have friends in places like Capitol Hill and the White House, who would weigh in to lend support and to influence Downing Street in seeing the wisdom in his political direction of travel. That Hume was right became clear in the outworkings of the Good Friday Agreement, when the US administration appointed one of their most senior and experienced politicians, Senator George Mitchell, to chair the negotiations, going even further with regular helpful interventions by President Bill Clinton himself at crucial moments during the negotiations.

***

John Hume, Garret FitzGerald and Margaret Thatcher had hoped that the 1985 Anglo-Irish Agreement would bolster the SDLP and middle-ground unionism, and diminish the relevance of Sinn Féin electorally. Clearly the British government had hoped that the improvement in Anglo-Irish relations flowing from this agreement would strengthen cross-border security and result in a greater crackdown on the IRA on both sides of the border. Unknown, however, to both governments, was the fact that key individuals in the IRA went into hiding as a result of that agreement, fearing a roundup of republican activists and, potentially, internment. Second and third lines of IRA leadership were put in place at that time as a buffer to such an eventuality. Sinn Féin continued to grow electorally at the same time as the IRA procured four major shipments of arms from Libya between August 1985 and 1986.

In spring 1985, in a radio interview, Gerry Adams challenged John Hume to meet Sinn Féin. Hume replied that he wanted to talk with those who really made the decisions in the republican movement – the IRA Army Council – to ask them to 'stop the violence'. Within days, the council had issued a public invitation to Hume. He agreed to the meeting. That was all we knew at the time – I learned later from Hume's wife, Pat, that his encounter with the IRA started with his being collected from his West End Park home in Derry and being driven to an unknown location in the Irish Republic. He was held there for twenty-eight hours, then he was told the meeting was about to take place. Three people arrived, one of whom described himself as a spokesman for the IRA. Just before the meeting commenced, Hume was informed it would be filmed. Hume said he did not approve of this, pointing out that he would have no control over any future use of the filmed material. The IRA spokesman said, 'Then the meeting is off.' John Hume arrived back at his home in the early hours of Sunday morning to the great relief of his family. Pat Hume spoke to me of the anxiety she and her family had felt at the time, not knowing what might happen to John or where he was. In spite of this experience, the SDLP leader was not deterred and decided he would try again to engage with the IRA and Sinn Féin when the next opportunity arose.

That opportunity came in the shape of the February 1987 election in the Republic of Ireland, which resulted in the formation of a coalition government with Charles Haughey at the helm. By now, Father Reid was regularly forwarding Haughey drafts of potential political avenues to end all violence in Northern Ireland and help Adams to lead the IRA away from the armed struggle. Father Reid's letter had impacted hugely on John Hume and, after the 1987 election, he asked Mark Durkan to meet the Clonard Monastery priest. Durkan undertook a series of meetings with Father Reid to lay the foundations for discussions with Hume. Knowing Father Reid as I did, Durkan's account of the Clonard priest's 'sermons' to him did not surprise me. 'He spoke in gospel terms, spoke of people being treated as lepers, spoke of how Jesus had always been prepared to speak to everybody. He said he believed intensely that the Church couldn't simply hide behind condemnation of the IRA – "nor of course can you people",' he told Durkan. Unlike so many other clergymen, Reid – facing daily violence in his community – did not hide his head in the sand.

Father Reid took part in a series of meetings with John and Pat Hume, and Mark Durkan, in Derry and Donegal. These meetings were the building blocks for secret talks that would later become known as the Hume–Adams talks when their occurrence was exposed. As so often happens, wee spuds grow big. Those initial encounters between Adams and Hume would lead to delegate meetings between the SDLP and Sinn Féin in 1988 but, unknown to the SDLP and the outside world, Haughey had arranged parallel secret talks south of the border between Fianna Fáil and Sinn Féin. When I mentioned those parallel talks, held in a Redemptorist monastery in Dundalk in 1988, to Haughey years later, he said, 'Ah – you know about that.' Raising his hand and wagging a finger, he added, 'Dodgy, dodgy with my background and the Arms Trial. If that had leaked out at the time ...'

When the SDLP–Sinn Féin delegate talks ran into the sand in 1988, John Hume told his colleagues he was reserving the right to continue dialogue with Gerry Adams on a 'one-to-one' basis. Hume told me he recognised in Adams a political openness and he felt the Sinn Féin leader was serious about moving forward 'politically'. He directly contrasted Adams with Danny Morrison, whom he found very hard-line and inflexible. Hume's discussions with Adams would be the start of an iterative process which would emerge as one of the building blocks of the 1993 Downing Street Declaration.

John Hume, along with many other politicians, was making peace in the shadow of the gunman and, like all SDLP politicians, did not have any police protection. He was under threat from republicans and loyalists, with hard-line loyalists alleging that he was part of 'a pan-nationalist front'. Following the SAS killings of eight members of the IRA in the Loughgall ambush of May 1987, furious republicans targeted the family home of the Humes. Pat and daughter Mo were there when their windows were pounded with ball bearings followed by a fusillade of firebombs, which turned the windows and Pat's car into fireballs. Thankfully, Pat and Mo escaped unharmed via the back of the house.

A short time after taking up office in 1989, Northern Ireland's new secretary of state, Peter Brooke, sought a meeting with Hume to get his overall assessment of the political situation in Northern Ireland. During this period, post-Anglo-Irish Agreement, unionists remained at loggerheads with the British administration. Brooke was keen to reconnect with unionism and to move forward in some structures involving all the major political parties in Northern Ireland. In November 1990, he made a statement of seismic importance about Britain's attitude towards Northern Ireland, when he stated in his Westminster constituency that Britain has 'no selfish strategic or economic interest' in Northern Ireland and would accept the unification of Ireland if consent should be forthcoming. Brooke told me that John Hume, with whom he had regular discussions at Westminster, wanted him to include 'no political interest' in his comment, but 'as a minister of the Crown, I could not say that'.

In the early nineties Hume had told Irish diplomat Seán Donlon the following: 'We have been at it for twenty-five years, we have tried everything, and nothing has worked.' According to Donlon, Hume argued that one of the reasons for this was because an important group of people were 'outside the tent rather than inside'. Hume 'talked about the difference between a cactus and a caucus and he said on a cactus all the pricks are on the outside. He said we've got to transmute or convert from having a cactus structure to a caucus structure.'

The Brooke statement impacted hugely, not just in Dublin but also in the upper echelons of republicanism, resonating particularly with party president Gerry Adams, who saw his utterance as one of the most important contributions to be delivered by a member of the British cabinet. Hume exploited Brooke's remarks, using them as a foundation for deepening his conversation with Adams. He underscored the fact that a British minister was now willing to state that his government would accept the unification of Ireland on the basis of consent.

In March 1991, Brooke called a new round of Northern Ireland talks. For the first time, he introduced the notion of 'three strands', the strands being relationships within Northern Ireland, relationships on the island of Ireland, and relationships between Ireland and Britain. This approach appealed to Hume: his analysis of how to solve the political deadlock was now being adopted as the Downing Street agenda. Brooke was replaced by Patrick Mayhew in 1992, who picked up where Brooke had left off with what became known as the Brooke–Mayhew talks. Brooke and Mayhew engaged in fresh political talks with unionists and nationalists but, unknown to the outside world, they were – with Prime Minister John Major – also up to their oxters in secret talks with the IRA (as I detail in chapter 7). Coincidentally, John Hume hoped that the secret talks he was having with Gerry Adams might merge down the road with the outcome of the Brooke–Mayhew discussions.

The government-sponsored talks which took place between April 1991 and November 1992 didn't get anywhere because of procedural difficulties in Strand One, i.e. relationships in Northern Ireland. For the British government, getting the unionists back on board after the Anglo-Irish Agreement was a problem plain for all to see, but what I didn't know at the time was that an internal battle was raging inside the SDLP. Despite my being a political anorak, obsessed with minutiae of political developments in Northern Ireland, as was often the case it was beneath the plimsoll line that some of the really big stories were developing.

Part of the British government bait for unionist involvement in the Brooke–Mayhew talks was having longer gaps between Anglo-Irish cross-border intergovernmental meetings, to which

Hume agreed. He met, however, with very significant resistance inside his own party from Seamus Mallon, Eddie McGrady and others, who argued that to allow a wider gap between meetings would amount to a 'hollowing out' of the structures put in place by the Anglo-Irish Agreement. They felt this suspension of meetings, even if only temporary, was precisely what the unionists had wanted.

I recently learned from Mark Durkan that one Saturday night back in 1992 he got a phone call from Pat Hume asking him to come over to the house. When he arrived, Pat informed him that John had drafted his resignation letter as party leader, but not as an MP. However, he told Durkan to start readying himself to stand for Westminster in the event of a general election. Hume had always known that, sooner or later, the Anglo-Irish Agreement would lead to a catharsis inside unionism. He hadn't ever thought otherwise, and he realised from the outset that the Anglo-Irish Agreement was not in itself a solution. When Durkan read Hume's resignation letter, he was quite taken aback at its tone. He told me, 'I argued why it was wrong to resign. I told John it was going against his own counsel of not "reacting to reaction".' Durkan insisted that Hume's resignation would potentially wreck everything, including the Hume–Adams talks. After further discussion, Hume agreed not to resign.

The outside world knew nothing about the dialogue between Adams and Hume until April 1993, when Derry republican Daisy Mules spotted Adams outside Hume's home on a Saturday morning. Daisy told former civil rights leader Eamonn McCann what she had seen and McCann, a journalist himself, called Ed Moloney, who was working for the *Sunday Tribune* at the time. Moloney, in turn, called Hume. Initially, the SDLP leader was reluctant to say anything but, according to Moloney, Hume called back minutes later and confirmed that talks were taking place between him and Adams. This disclosure came close to causing an earthquake in politics in both Northern Ireland and the Republic. There was uproar in unionist circles. UUP leader Jim Molyneaux accused Mr Hume of 'supping with the devil'. On learning of the talks, the first thing that came into my head was, damn it, why didn't I get that story? When I got over my disappointment, I recognised that once more it was Hume thinking long-term rather than short-term. He knew the risks of engaging directly with Adams but was prepared to do it for the sake of peace.

Like everybody else in the community at that point in time, I could see nothing happening that indicated to me that peace was on the horizon. There was a growing number of loyalist attacks on republicans. This escalation in violence caused a no-holds-barred response from the IRA. At lunchtime on 23 October 1993, two IRA members disguised as delivery men carried a bomb into Frizzell's fish shop on the Shankill Road in Belfast. It was a Saturday afternoon and the district was bustling with shoppers. The bomb detonated prematurely, killing ten people and injuring more than fifty. A police contact had tipped me off that day that one of the bombers had been killed in the explosion. I called a senior republican to ask if this was true. There was a sharp intake of breath at the other end of the phone.

That afternoon, I raced to the Mater Hospital and saw the distress and anger of the friends and families of those who had been killed. Such was their manifest outrage, I was actually afraid I might get beaten up. The IRA claimed to have been targeting the leadership of the UDA, who met in an office above Frizzell's. In fact, they weren't there at the time. The bombing mission was reckless in the extreme – targeting that area on a busy Saturday afternoon, with hundreds of people shopping and going about their business.

In June 1995, former IRA hunger striker and republican activist, Pat 'Beag' McGeown, who died in 1996, gave me an insight into the thinking of the IRA leadership in carrying out the Shankill Road bombing: 'Our people were under pressure with regards to loyalist assassinations. It was a case of having to do something. The opportunity and unity appeared to exist to take out the command staff of the Ulster Freedom Fighters [UFF], the paramilitary death units within the UDA. It would have had to go through Belfast Brigade to the Army Council. It was in line with IRA policy. The increase in loyalist attacks led to action like this. Before Shankill the intensity of sectarian killings was as bad as you were going to get.'

I asked McGeown, 'Why do this before an IRA ceasefire?'

His response was, 'We were saying the ceasefire was coming from a position of strength. We were saying it wasn't a case of the IRA being burnt out. Consultation went from top to bottom. People from GHQ talked to everybody. Our community expected the IRA to be the defenders and it expected the IRA to exact a price for heavy loyalist assassinations.'

Another IRA source, when asked about the rationale of the Shankill Road bombing, said, 'A decision was taken to take the head off the snake.'

Thomas Begley was the name of the bomber who had been blown up by his own device in Frizzell's. I had been around republicanism long enough to know that Gerry Adams had little or no option but to be seen at his funeral. That said, it didn't matter what I thought – the image of Adams carrying the coffin sent shockwaves through Downing Street and beyond. The recklessness of the IRA planting a bomb in the loyalist heartland of the Shankill – and the attendant photo of Adams bearing the coffin at the funeral of one of the bombers – came just six months after the revelation that Hume was in talks with Adams. The Shankill bomb only served to intensify the hostility towards Hume, not just from unionism and loyalism, but also from within his own party and from sections of the media, including in Dublin. Some of the highest-profile columnists in the Irish Republic, including Conor Cruise O'Brien and Eamon Dunphy, turned on Hume. Hume had this message for his detractors: 'I don't care two balls of roasted snow about the criticism.'

We all knew that retaliation for the Shankill bombing was inevitable – it was only a matter of time. On 30 October 1993, members of the UFF entered a crowded pub in Greysteel in County Derry and opened fire. Eight people were killed and nineteen others injured. The UFF claimed responsibility for the attack and said it was in revenge for the Shankill Road bombing.

John Hume was in London when I called him for a response. He was shattered. I continued to update him throughout the evening as the scale of what had happened became clear. The strain on him broke through in a very public way during the funeral of one of the Greysteel victims. To see Hume in floods of tears on our TV screens that evening was heartbreaking. It brought tears to my eyes; I suspect the many other people who were desperate for peace felt the same. Not long before she died, Pat Hume told me, 'I asked John after Greysteel to rethink his talks with Gerry Adams because the pressure was so great at that time. John told me, "I've started and I will continue."' She added, 'He didn't give another thought to it. He could see the big picture – I only see small pictures.'

***

On 15 December 1993, John Major and Albert Reynolds signed the Downing Street Declaration. It affirmed both the right of the people of Ireland to self-determination and that Northern Ireland would be transferred to the Republic of Ireland from the United Kingdom only if a majority of its population was in favour of such a move. It also included, as part of the so-called 'Irish dimension', the principle of consent that the people of the island of Ireland had the exclusive right to solve the issues between North and South by mutual consent.

Sinn Féin organised a special conference in Letterkenny, County Donegal, on Sunday 24 July 1994 to consider the Declaration. At that time, Patrick McGrory, who had acted as legal advisor to Gerry Adams for decades, said in response to it, 'Only madmen make war for fun.' On arrival in the car park of the hotel where the conference was taking place, Mitchel McLaughlin, one of Sinn Féin's key negotiators, divulged a critical piece of information. He told me that in the weeks leading up to the conference, every single IRA unit in the country had been consulted, sounded out and briefed. He added, 'Be careful in what you are saying. There could be a silver lining in there.' He didn't expand, and it left me with a considerable puzzle as to what he actually meant. Of course, now we know that the silver lining was that there was enough in the Downing Street Declaration to justify probing both the British and Irish governments further on the potential in the agreement, in particular the fact that it was now in black and white that the people on the island of Ireland had the right to self-determination.

Gerry Adams addressed the July conference. He is reported to have said that the Downing Street Declaration 'suggests a potentially significant change in the approach of the governments to resolving the conflict in Ireland, and we welcome this. But it does not deal adequately with some of the core issues, and this is crucial.' The overall impression that emerged from the conference was that the attendees were critical of the declaration, and so it was interpreted as a rejection of the declaration and, thus, of peace.

Sean Farren, who was with Hume that Sunday evening on holiday in France, told me of the SDLP leader's overt anxiety about the potential outcome of the conference, which was punctuated by phone calls to the Department of Foreign Affairs in Dublin. Despite the perceived lack of enthusiasm from Sinn Féin, Hume issued a hopeful statement at the end of the conference. Taoiseach Albert Reynolds, too, struck a positive note but knew other issues needed attention on the road to a ceasefire. What was telling though was that aide to Reynolds, Dr Martin Mansergh, who probably knew the mindset of republicans better than most through Father Alec Reid and Gerry Adams, asked the British government not to be 'rebarbative' in its response to the outcome of Letterkenny. That said, such was the scale of the gloom in the aftermath of the Sinn Féin delegate meeting in Donegal that it even got to Reynolds. He remembers it as one of his darkest moments and told me, 'I was saying one thing and everyone was saying the opposite to me, including a lot of members of my own party.' As for myself, I was travelling in hope that the IRA would stop the violence, but I had been around long enough to know that their journey to peace was always going to be very bumpy.

In early August 1994, Danny Morrison was out on temporary release from the Maze Prison where he was serving eight years, having been convicted in 1990 of false imprisonment and conspiracy to murder an informer called Sandy Lynch. (This conviction was overturned in 2008, when Lord Chief Justice Brian Kerr found the convictions to be unsafe.) Standing in the Sinn Féin bookshop on the Falls Road in West Belfast to promote the new novel that he had written in jail, he agreed to take some questions from reporters. As part of the reply to a question on the current state of politics, Morrison remarked, 'That's why an alternative strategy to armed struggle is being examined.' I seized upon what he had just said, and I could see from the stricken face of the Sinn Féin head of publicity, Richard McAuley, that he was secretly asking himself, 'Which of the two of them – Morrison for dropping a clanger or Mallie for latching on to it – is the bigger bastard?' That comment was a defining one, and I gave it maximum attention in my reports that afternoon.

This changing attitude of the IRA was confirmed to me on 18 August 1994, when I went to see the vice-president of Sinn Féin, Martin McGuinness, at his home in Derry. I spent several hours with him. My visit took place against a backdrop of heavy speculation about an IRA ceasefire. In an unguarded conversation, we discussed violence at length. I spelled out to McGuinness that with my background and upbringing as a Catholic, and as a human being, I was totally opposed to violence being used against my fellow human beings. McGuinness stared at me and said, 'How do you think I feel?' I was taken aback. It felt as if he had been waiting to get an opportunity to say this. I knew it was not likely he would tell me that the IRA ceasefire would take place in one week, two weeks or even three weeks but, as I was leaving, I said to him, 'Would it be safe for me to be out of town in the next fortnight?' He looked straight at me with that stare of his and said, 'If I were you, I would not be out of town in the next few weeks.' I said goodbye and headed for Belfast with a lot on my mind. Martin McGuinness had said nothing, but he had said everything.

That night, I happened to walk into the Wellington Park Hotel in South Belfast. I noticed John Hume sitting alone on the long seat opposite the reception area, looking decidedly crestfallen. When I said hello, he lifted his head and said, 'What do you think, Eamonn?' He was clearly asking me did I think there was going to be an IRA ceasefire. I was taken aback. I couldn't believe that Hume was asking my opinion. He had been my family's reference point politically, all our lives. It was he who carried the torch for my generation, which was opposed to violence for political ends. I habitually referred to him to inform myself about what was going on. His question put me in a difficult position. Martin McGuinness' comment that I should not be out of Northern Ireland in the coming weeks was probably one of the most important pieces of news in the Western world, but I had to guard against trading information. I fell back on a much-used South Armagh saying in answering Hume. 'Keep the faith,' I said. He replied, 'Do you think so?' I repeated, 'Keep the faith,' and I walked away.

Unknown to me, just an hour earlier, Hume had been eviscerated by many of the big beasts in his party. The homes of leading SDLP members were being regularly attacked by loyalists and Hume's ongoing talks with Adams were being promoted as a pan-nationalist front. These issues were raised at that meeting, resulting in Hume feeling isolated within his own party for the first time, with only a handful of supporters backing him. Going home in the car that night with Mark Durkan, Hume once again talked about resigning, shattered as a result of what had happened to him at the meeting. Despite this talk, Durkan later told me he had known his leader was going to Dublin the next morning with Pat and that she would put an end to all the talk about quitting. He was right, and Hume's decision to continue the talks with Adams, despite the opposition from within his own party, proved to be a wise course of action.

Less than two weeks later, on 31 August 1994, the IRA declared a cessation of all militant activity. Hume confounded his critics and left egg on a lot of faces in journalism and on the faces of Dublin commentators in Sunday newspapers who had crucified him over his engagement with Adams. His place in history was secured. He had entered the lion's den and delivered for the people of this island.

***

On that morning of 31 August, BBC journalist Brian Rowan and I had received separate phone calls from a republican source known to us both. We were advised where we should go to meet an IRA contact. Given what McGuinness had said to me, I felt it in my waters that we were going to be given the news for which we had been hoping. Potentially, we would be living an Angel Gabriel experience – receiving the good news from the messenger.

To our surprise, in the appointed West Belfast restaurant, we met a young woman – I'd met other IRA representatives in the past and they had all been men. She handed us a piece of paper with this carefully drafted statement:

Irish Republican Army (IRA) Ceasefire Statement, 31 August 1994

Recognising the potential of the current situation and in order to enhance the democratic process and underlying our definitive commitment to its success, the leadership of the IRA have decided that as of midnight, August 31, there will be a complete cessation of military operations. All our units have been instructed accordingly. At this crossroads the leadership of the IRA salutes and commends our volunteers, other activists, our supporters and the political prisoners who have sustained the struggle against all odds for the past 25 years. Your courage, determination and sacrifice have demonstrated that the freedom and the desire for peace based on a just and lasting settlement cannot be crushed. We remember all those who have died for Irish freedom and we reiterate our commitment to our republican objectives. Our struggle has seen many gains and advances made by nationalists and for the democratic position. We believe that an opportunity to secure a just and lasting settlement has been created. We are therefore entering into a new situation in a spirit of determination and confidence, determined that the injustices which created this conflict will be removed and confident in the strength and justice of our struggle to achieve this. We note that the Downing Street Declaration is not a solution, nor was it presented as such by its authors. A solution will only be found as a result of inclusive negotiations. Others, not the least the British government, have a duty to face up to their responsibilities. It is our desire to significantly contribute to the creation of a climate which will encourage this. We urge everyone to approach this new situation with energy, determination and patience.

How could I not rejoice on reading this news, which hopefully marked the end of thirty years of violence? It was also potentially the biggest story in the world that day. Within minutes, Brian and I were spreading the historic message across the globe. The life blood of any journalist is getting a scoop. Nothing compared to this story, which was a game-changer for the lives of everyone on these islands.

Then, on 13 October, the Combined Loyalist Military Command (CLMC) delivered its ceasefire statement. That press conference had its own potency and the fact that the father figure of loyalism, Gusty Spence, delivered the ceasefire statement afforded it incontrovertible weight. I was with Brian Rowan that morning also. It seemed to me we had been 'soldiering' together longer than many of the combatants. The loyalist ceasefire statement read:

After a widespread consultative process initiated by representations from the Ulster Democratic and Progressive

Unionist Parties, and after having received confirmation and guarantees in relation to Northern Ireland's constitutional position within the United Kingdom, as well as other assurances, and, in the belief that the democratically expressed wishes of the greater number of people in Northern Ireland will be respected and upheld, the CLMC will universally cease all operational hostilities as from 12 midnight on Thursday 13th October 1994. The permanence of our ceasefire will be completely dependent upon the continued cessation of all nationalist/republican violence, the sole responsibility for a return to War lies with them. In the genuine hope that this peace will be permanent, we take the opportunity to pay homage to all our Fighters, Commandos and Volunteers who paid the supreme sacrifice. They did not die in vain. The Union is safe. To our physically and mentally wounded who have served Ulster so unselfishly, we wish a speedy recovery, and to the relatives of these men and women, we pledge our continued moral and practical support.

To our prisoners who have undergone so much deprivation and degradation with great courage and forbearance, we solemnly promise to leave no stone unturned to secure their freedom. To our serving officers, NCOs and personnel, we extend our eternal gratitude for their obedience of orders, for their ingenuity, resilience and good humour in the most trying of circumstances, and we commend them for their courageous fortitude and unshakeable faith over the long years of armed confrontation. In all sincerity, we offer to the loved ones of all innocent victims over the past twenty years, abject and true remorse. No words of ours will compensate for the intolerable suffering they have undergone during the conflict. Let us firmly resolve to respect our differing views of freedom, culture and aspiration and never again permit our political circumstances to degenerate into bloody warfare. We are on the threshold of a new and exciting beginning with our battles in future being political battles, fought on the side of honesty, decency and democracy against the negativity of mistrust, misunderstanding and malevolence, so that, together, we can bring forth a wholesome society in which our children, and their children, will know the meaning of true peace.

What jumped out at me in this loyalist statement were the words: 'In all sincerity, we offer to the loved ones of all innocent victims over the past twenty years, abject and true remorse. No words of ours will compensate for the intolerable suffering they have undergone during the conflict.' Nothing in the IRA ceasefire statement matched the clarity articulated in the loyalist statement, and this was conspicuous, especially to the unionist and loyalist community.

∗ ∗ ∗

Looking back on those days of my frontline journalism and considering where I went and the people with whom I was meeting in both IRA and loyalist circles, I can incontrovertibly say, quoting my favourite Irish poet, Patrick Kavanagh, 'I have lived in important places, times when great events were decided.' Pat Hume was modest in telling me that she only saw 'small pictures' and that John saw 'big pictures'. Her husband had written his name indelibly in the pages of history.

John Hume ended up a broken man in the service of all the people of Northern Ireland. He stood virtually alone aboard the deck when nearly everybody else around him on the boat was jumping off, fearing they would become contaminated through contact with Sinn Féin President Gerry Adams. Hume defied popular opinion and fought the great fight to help Adams to realise the cessation of violence on 31 August 1994.

There are two types of journalists, as I see it, in my profession: those who like being on the inside working out and those on the outside working in. I like mould breakers, single-mindedness, people with courage who show leadership. That leadership can manifest itself in any and every sphere of life, regardless of the background of people, rich or poor. It is having a sense of humanity and concern for those less well-off than oneself – and 'less well-off' covers a wide spectrum of factors. People with wealth are often visited with the biggest crosses.

Down the years in Northern Ireland, despite everything that was happening, I met some remarkable people and I learned an awful lot from some good people – people like Mo Mowlam, the former Northern Ireland secretary of state, who showed me not to be too judgemental, to find out for myself the worth of a person. I often stood back and admired Mo, whether she was in the company of a loyalist known by me to be part of a paramilitary organisation or a republican equally known by me to be part of a paramilitary organisation. She treated each individual with respect, seeking out the good within the soul of that person. Some people didn't like this, but courage and leadership quite often break through when least expected.

In this I am thinking of Alan McBride, who lost his wife and father-in-law in Frizzell's fish shop in the IRA bombing on that fatal Saturday afternoon on the Shankill Road. Today, Alan, who has every good reason to be bitter, reaches out his hand to those who would have been deemed his enemies. Here is a man who went and met Gerry Adams, the leader of republicanism, synonymous in the eyes of so many unionists and Protestants with the IRA and the totality of republicanism. Indeed, speaking with me one day in Parliament Buildings about Adams, former UUP leader David Trimble described the Sinn Féin president as 'the awfulest human being I have ever known'. Yet Alan McBride went and met Adams, teaching himself to be more forgiving and understanding of the human condition of others.

Other figures who have stood up and led from the front throughout the Troubles included people like Portadown man Michael McGoldrick, whose son, Michael, was shot dead during the standoff at Drumcree in Portadown. He too said that he forgave his son's killers.

One of the most impressive people I have met in public life, a man whom I interviewed a number of times, was Gordon Wilson, a Protestant who lost his daughter Marie in the Enniskillen bombing on Remembrance Day on 8 November 1987. The immortal words, 'Daddy, I love you very much', uttered by Marie before she died, were words which reverberated around the world. Gordon Wilson said, 'I miss my daughter and we shall all miss her, but I bear no ill will, I bear no grudge. I shall pray for those people tonight and every night.' That is leadership. That is courage. That is humanity writ large.

We had other manifestations down through the Troubles

of greatness, of leadership, of courage in the persons of Father Alec Reid and Father Gerry Reynolds, who crossed the divide to share in grief and to mourn with the family, for example, of Raymond Smallwoods, killed by the IRA. Smallwoods was a leading member of the UDA. Another exemplar was Presbyterian Minister Ken Newell, who spoke to me about meeting members of the IRA. He talked about journeying into their hearts at the same time as the IRA was killing RUC members of his congregation.

One other shining star to emerge within the Protestant unionist community was the Reverend William Bingham, chaplain to the Orange Order in Armagh, who stood up and was counted during the standoff at Drumcree between the Orangemen and the police, at a time when the Portadown Orange Order was determined to do what it always did in July – to parade from Carleton Street Orange Hall in Portadown to Drumcree church, marching on their return via the Garvaghy Road in Portadown, a Catholic nationalist area. Their stance was do or die. From 1995 through to 2000, like the hunger strike in 1981, the annual Drumcree Orange march tore the community in Northern Ireland apart – triggering an exodus of nationalists and Catholics to the Continent, Donegal or to the west of Ireland for the month of July. People would have done anything to avoid the upheaval and disruption taking place across Northern Ireland in support of the Orangemen, who wanted to continue marching where they had marched for hundreds of years, through Catholic areas of Portadown. In 1998, confronted with what he deemed unacceptable, William Bingham decided to take a stand. He later told me that in the lead-up to that year's Drumcree standoff:

For two or three weeks before the Garvaghy Road/Drum-cree parade, I had been warning if the Parades Commission ruled against Portadown Orange, then the RUC could not back down. The response of the Portadown district Orange was that it was a 'fight to the death', meaning body bags, they would stay there and they would die or be killed: that was their idea of an exit strategy.

I argued there should be an exit strategy to enable us to walk away with our heads held high, our honour intact. I suggested if the Parades Commission ruled against us then we shouldn't leave Carleton Street Orange Hall [the headquarters of the Orange in Portadown], because I felt we could keep more control over the situation, taking the view that unless we could be in control we shouldn't protest and I feared there would be problems in the field at Drumcree. I took the view we should stay in Carleton Street until we were clear to march the whole route. I lost the argument.

During the standoff in 1998 between the Orange and the RUC in Portadown, when the members of the security services lined up almost on a nightly basis from Sunday 5 July to block the return leg down the Garvaghy Road, the police came under extraordinary pressure. In the early hours of 12 July 1998, in Ballymoney, at the height of the standoff, three Catholic children – Richard (11), Mark (10) and Jason (9) Quinn – were burned to death in their home when it was petrol bombed in a sectarian attack by loyalists. The UVF were accused of the bomb attack. The Reverend Bingham recalled:

On the Sunday night [5 July] in the field I saw real venom towards the RUC and I didn't like it. I wasn't there on Wednesday night because I went to Downing Street. Then on Thursday night there was the blast bomb attack on the police. I stood and watched five or six thousand people down by the barbed wire cheering at what had happened. I said to myself 'this is not about Orangeism, this is evil'.

At a meeting of the Executive on Friday morning I made my feelings known. I felt if we couldn't control what was going on we should disperse and establish a peace camp, a Greenham Common type base manned by 14–15 people. I spoke to Brendan McAllister of Mediation Network and I told him I was thinking of saying something publicly. He advised me to stay within the camp. On Friday night the police were fired upon. Then I went to a funeral on Saturday. I wasn't at Drumcree, but I was praying, and I started to think about my sermon for Sunday morning. I was to address two congregations in two churches. In the meantime there had been incidents in the Lurgan area as all the other things were going on. On Sunday morning I woke up and I heard what had happened at Ballymoney [to the three Quinn boys].

I decided I was going to say something, I couldn't hold back any more.

I had a call from my cousin in Markethill, with whom I spent a lot of time. Lewis is a solicitor there. He called me and said: 'William, you have to say something. You have got to say something.' A former moderator of the Presbyterian Church, David McCaughey from Kilkeel also called me and urged me to say something.

Above: The class of 1970, Abbey CBS, university and teacher-training entrants, with me in the bottom left corner. (Courtesy of the *Newry Reporter*)

Left: Detta dressed up for a ball.

Detta and I on our engagement in autumn 1975.

The burning of my news car during a republican rally in West Belfast in August 1984.
(© Pacemaker)

Former IRA Chief of Staff Ruairí Ó Brádaigh leading a walk-out from a Sinn Féin Ard-Fheis in 1986 after the party decided to end abstentionism from Dáil Éireann.

Interviewing Northern Ireland Secretary of State Douglas Hurd during his tenure in 1984–5.

Interrogating former Labour Party leader Michael Foot in Blackpool in the early eighties.

Face to face with Northern Ireland Secretary of State Tom King in 1985.

A media scrum with SDLP leader John Hume taking questions during the 1988
Good Friday Agreement negotiations.

Happy memories of exchanges in 1998 with Northern Ireland Secretary of State
Mo Mowlam at the time of the signing of the Good Friday Agreement.

US President Bill Clinton trying on my son Michael's neon-blue sunglasses in
Enniskillen in 2002. (Courtesy of Harrison Photography)

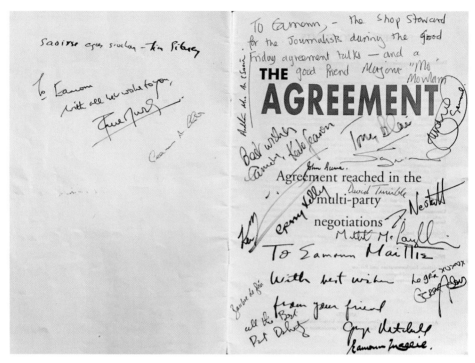

The signatures of the history-makers of the Good Friday Agreement.

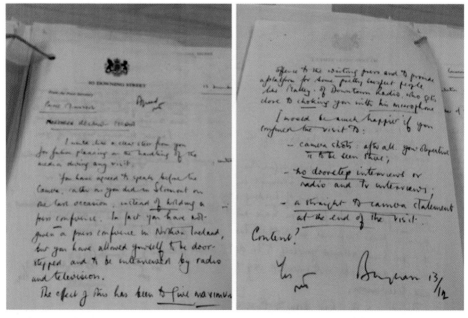

A handwritten letter of 1983 to Prime Minister Margaret Thatcher from her director
of communications recommending that she should blackball me on future visits to
Northern Ireland.

Former DUP leader Ian Paisley proudly showing me his father's wooden training rifle.
He was a member of Carson's UVF army of 1910–22.
(© Press Eye Photography)

Interviewing former Prime Minister Tony Blair for UTV's *Eamonn Mallie: Face to Face with ...* (© UTV/Neil Genower Photography)

A portrait of me painted by Colin Davidson.
(© Colin Davidson)

Ciara, Laura-Kate and Michael on Ciara's wedding day in 2004.

It should be noted that Reverend William Bingham and his family were neighbours of the late Seamus Mallon MP, and Mallon spoke warmly to me about them as neighbours. I gathered from Mallon he had been in touch with the Reverend Bingham during this period. The Reverend Bingham continued:

I prayed on Sunday morning about what I was going to say. I phoned Downing Street and was put through to Jonathan Powell and I told him what I was going to say. I wanted confirmation for what I was going to say ... I tried to phone Denis Watson [the Order's grand master in County Armagh]. I got his mobile and his answer machine and left a message for him, telling him what I intended saying.

I called UTV and the BBC and I think they went live on BBC News 24. At the field [in Tyrone, where the annual 12 July gathering was held] it was difficult. I was more worried for my children. I didn't want anything to happen to me in front of my children. When I was making my way to the field in Tyrone an Orangeman grabbed me by the throat and the collar and pushed me into the hedge. My friends moved in and stopped them from giving me a kicking. When I was going up to the podium, I was warned I would be heckled if I said anything. My reply was: 'No one would stop me speaking the word of the Lord Jesus Christ.'

When I delivered my address, I stuck to a biblical address. I didn't refer to anything political. I didn't want to give them any excuse to have a go at me or to get any opening. When I had finished preaching a man stepped forward and attacked me, claiming I had brought an IRA man to the Orange field. I didn't know 'he' [O'Callaghan] was there. I was nervous as I spoke and I worried because of what happened. Then my own people moved in to protect me, lots of people came up to congratulate me. Many told me afterwards that they were praying during the services on Sunday that I would say something.

Denis Watson, a leading Orangeman, asked me to join him for a meal at lunchtime with Ruth Dudley Edwards, the well-known journalist, who had in her company former IRA man Sean O'Callaghan. I didn't arrange for Sean O'Callaghan to meet me.

The Reverend Bingham told me:

I said to myself what was going on in the field at Drumcree – this isn't Christian, this is paganism, this is nothing to do with Christianity.

With regards to the Orange Order, I said to myself it can do two things; destroy itself or reform. I asked myself is it capable of reform? Has it the capacity for reform? I concluded right now it is going down the tubes.

In a visionary comment on the deaths of the Quinn boys, the Reverend Bingham said, 'No road is worth the life, let alone the lives of three little boys.'

The Reverend William Bingham said a fifteen-minute walk down Garvaghy Road would be 'a hollow victory following the killings in Ballymoney'. This was leadership.

Chapter Seven

Secret Talks

SOMETIMES THERE IS MYSTERY about journalism; sometimes there is a perception that politicians or people in power wilfully leak a story to a journalist. Although this does happen, uncovering a good story is more often the result of serendipity, accident or a seemingly unimportant meeting or conversation.

So, in 1988, when I got a call from Pádraig O'Malley – a professor at the University of Massachusetts, who specialised in the problems of divided societies – inviting me to lunch in Belfast, I accepted. During the meal, Pádraig asked what I knew about Duisburg. 'What?' I replied. 'Secret talks have been taking place in Duisburg in Germany,' he said. 'They started in 1985, stuttered, then continued in '87. The most recent talks took place this year.' Pádraig went on to tell me that among the representatives at these talks were Peter Robinson (Democratic Unionist Party – DUP), Austin Currie (SDLP), Jack Allen (UUP) and Gordon Mawhinney (Alliance). Father Alec Reid was also there, as was a German clergyman.

I knew this was a big story and I couldn't wait to get away from the table to start working on it. As soon as I was back at my desk, I started to make some calls. I phoned Peter Robinson, who was very uncomplicated. He confirmed that he had been there but added, 'Have your thirty seconds of glory if you want to but you might spoil something that's growing.' Next, I called Austin Currie, who was gracious and also confirmed his attendance. By contrast, Jack Allen categorically denied knowing anything about Duisburg.

As I geared up to write the story, I told Detta about it. She listened carefully. Our children were very young at the time. She said, 'Do you never think that we're rearing children, and that maybe there's a chance here for peace, and that you broadcasting this story might ruin it?' It was a sobering moment. I didn't run the story.

Some weeks later, I was watching the BBC news, as usual, and Denis Murray was giving the Duisburg story his best, and showing footage of the complex where the talks had been held. I was sick as a parrot looking at the story I'd been working on weeks earlier, but I also felt that the time allocated to the Duisburg discussions by the BBC was disproportionate. In essence, those talks ended up going up in a puff of smoke.

✳ ✳ ✳

In early March 1993, I was listening to the evening news on BBC Radio Ulster, during which Robin Eames, Archbishop of Armagh and Primate of All Ireland, was interviewed. I was fascinated by what he was saying – this was the second time that I had heard him hinting at something going on. I had previously considered Dr Eames to be narrow in his political thinking, though in what he had said recently I felt he was opening up another front, conceivably foreign even to himself, and it was this that triggered my curiosity. I didn't feel we had a very good relationship, but nonetheless I rang him and told him that I had just been listening to him on the radio, and that I found what he was saying very interesting. He surprised me by asking me to come and see him at his home in Armagh. I spent two hours there and I probed him about his oblique references on the radio. He was not very forthcoming but did say, 'Very few people know about it.' He didn't expand on this and I knew it would not be prudent to push him, but that remark sharpened my interest even more – I felt it confirmed that something was developing between the government and paramilitary groups.

Parting company with the archbishop, I had a deep suspicion that secret talks might be taking place involving the British government and republicans, but it was not enough. Mindful of the sensitivity of the story, I had to stand it up with incontrovertible facts. I embarked on a series of phone calls, ringing the usual conspiratorial types within unionism – UUP party leader Jim Molyneaux, members of the DUP and others. I drew a blank. Republicans were making no comment either. I didn't give up. Come autumn 1993, a republican source hinted to me about the existence of contact between republicans and the government. I had to pledge I would not ever reveal the identity of that individual.

Armed with my latest nugget of information, I called the NIO press office to ask whether the government had been engaged in talks with republicans. The response was that they had no knowledge of such talks or meetings – 'The secretary of state has made his opinion on talking to Sinn Féin very clear on many occasions.' I posed the same question to the Downing Street Press Office and Jonathan Haslam, the spokesperson for the government, who later became John Major's director of communications, responded. 'It seems like fantasy to me,' he said. 'We have made clear on many occasions that we don't speak to those who carry out or advocate or condone violence to further their political aims.' Haslam added in conversation that he had spoken to the NIO and was told, 'This twaddle was around a lot over the summer.'

This was a lonely road for me as a journalist. I had visions of myself being sued for accusing the secretary of state of lying, and sitting in court listening to affidavits or depositions being read out by the attorney general in his defence. Nonetheless, I was determined that I was going to the end of the road in pursuit of this story. Archbishop Eames had started the hare running for me; in late autumn 1993 the scent was growing stronger.

By now, I had been advised by my republican source that it might be worth my while to speak to the Reverend William McCrea, the DUP MP who lived in Magherafelt. I called him on 11 November 1993. When I asked him if he had heard about any contact between the IRA, Sinn Féin and republicans and the British government, he replied, 'I have a source who has told me the British government right from the top and right to the top of the republican movement are meeting and are in contact.' He added that the information had come to him prior to the Shankill Road bombing, which took place on 23 October 1993. McCrea disclosed to me that he had been in his office at Westminster, which he shared with Ian Paisley, when the phone rang and a person with a cultured voice asked to speak to Mr Paisley. McCrea told the person on the line who he was and that Paisley was not there at that moment. 'The caller reassured me that there definitely was contact right to the top and gave me a commitment that he would provide evidence for me that these communications were happening.' McCrea, with whom I always got on well, told me on the phone that he was expecting to have some hard evidence of the communications soon. It was something of a surprise that the anonymous caller opted to impart this critical message to McCrea, the mid-Ulster MP, rather than Paisley.

That afternoon, I was in my study at home. I had continued to ask ministers and press officers non-stop about these alleged contacts and was being shot down in flames again and again. Every time I saw Patrick Mayhew, I asked him, 'Are you in contact with Sinn Féin or the IRA?' I was desperate to get my hands on the smoking gun. Now, McCrea was on the other end of the phone confirming to me that he had collected a document, which he agreed to fax to me. My heart was thumping as the fax came through. I thanked McCrea and started to read:

The following instructions should be delivered orally to [name deleted] when you hand over annexe C in written form. In handing over this written message you need make no bones about the fact that it is a written message that you are handing over. You should emphasise that this process is fraught with difficulties for the British Government, as must be obvious. They are nevertheless prepared to tackle these and accept the risks that they entail. But it must be recognised that all acts of violence hereafter could only enhance these difficulties and risks, quite conceivably to the point when the process would be destroyed. If that were to occur the British Government would consider that a potentially historic opportunity had been squandered. The paper gives out substantive advice in response to the initial message. As it makes clear we wish to establish whether this provides a basis for a way forward. We, on our side, are ready to answer any specific questions or give further explanation. You should also emphasise to your interlocutor the British Government's acknowledgement that all of those involved share a responsibility to work to end the conflict. We agree on the need for a healing process. We wish to take a positive view of these developments and hope that it will be possible to continue to do so. You should be aware that the above has been personally approved by SOSNI [secretary of state for Northern Ireland]. In fact all but the first sentence of the first paragraph is his own wording. In other words, it is not negotiable.

Every instinct in my waters told me that this document originated with the British government and was clearly designed to convey a very specific message to the republican movement. This was incontrovertible evidence of government–IRA communication, but I had to substantiate it. McCrea was also nervous and wanted to have the document authenticated.

On 22 November, Patrick Mayhew was going to plant a tree at Malone House in South Belfast. Now that I had what would become known as Mayhew's 'speaking note', I decided I would raise my game. I asked Billy Millar – a press officer and an old friend of mine – to share a number of 'buzz words' from the document with the secretary of state's private office before the event at Malone House. Years later, Billy told me that he drafted a memo covering the conversation we had and passed the details to his director of communications in the NIO, Andy Wood. Pandemonium followed. Billy told me, 'At that moment they knew you had them.' However, at the time, on the ground, it felt as though nothing had changed. I'd asked Mayhew the same question so many times by this point that most of my journalistic colleagues thought I was off my trolley. On this occasion, I asked Mark Lyons of ITN to put my now-familiar question to him. Mayhew gave his stock reply.

So, I was still left with a dilemma: how to authenticate the document in my possession. I decided to get in touch with a retired civil servant, Dr George Quigley. I had known George down the years and I considered him an enlightened, visionary man. I asked him if he would take a look at this document and advise me as to its authenticity. He decided against doing so, saying, 'I am out of it now, Eamonn. I am not familiar with the goings-on and I would prefer not to get involved.' I decided to try instead a senior QC, James McSparran, whom I had known for a long time and who had a lifetime's experience of government documents. He read the document with great attention, lifted his head and said, 'Eamonn, I would say it's 1,000 per cent authentic, but you can't use it.' I reminded him that I had come for an opinion about the document, not for editorial advice about what I should do with it.

I left satisfied as to the authenticity of the document, but I still needed further clarification and reassurance – if I got this wrong my career would be left hanging in the balance. I drove to Derry to meet John Hume to get his take. I met him in a pub in the city centre and showed him the text. He fell back in his seat as if he had just been hit by a hammer. John had no doubt about the authenticity of this document but was astonished by it. He had been involved in talks with Gerry Adams for several years before details came into the public domain in April 1993, but neither the republicans nor the British had revealed to him that there was another game being played out in the background.

With James McSparran and John Hume both so certain of the bona fides of the document in my possession, I decided to break cover and to publish what I knew. This was one of the biggest stories of my career and I knew it was of international importance. On Thursday 25 November, I called Mary Holland, *The Observer*'s Ireland correspondent – I was friendly with her as I regularly freelanced for the paper. I briefed Mary on the substance of my breaking story and she urged me to call the paper's managing editor, John Price, and fill him in on what I had. When I told Price, he became very excited and asked me to forward a written memo to him as soon as possible outlining the content of my story. I had a number of conversations over the next twenty-four hours, and I could tell that he knew that he had a front-page story. Price then consulted his editor, Donald Telford, and apprised political editor Tony Bevins of my scoop. Bevins in turn went straight to the House of Commons to speak to Michael Ancram, Patrick Mayhew's deputy.

We know now that by Saturday morning, Downing Street was in crisis mode. An insider told me that the Cabinet Office was in a flap and hastily arranged a meeting to work out a strategy on how to handle the story that was going to break in *The Observer* the next day. Those present were Andy Wood, director of communications in the NIO; Robin Butler, Cabinet secretary; Rod Lyne from the Cabinet Office; Gus O'Donnell, Major's press secretary; Patrick Mayhew; Michael

Ancram; Quentin Thomas, deputy to Sir John Chilcot, the NIO permanent secretary; and Jonathan Stephens, also of the NIO. The seniority of the people at that gathering was a measure of the gravity of the situation. There was a sense of panic. How had this most secret of documents got into the public domain? There was an acceptance that to deny contact would not be prudent, but the question was how to frame the government's contention that it was not talking 'to terrorists' but rather communicating with republicans through messengers.

The Observer was on a high, with its front-page story. When the paper hit the streets, the headline screamed, 'Major's secret links with IRA leadership revealed'. There were three names on the story: Tony Bevins', Mary Holland's and mine. My ego was bruised because I wasn't the sole name on the article, and I decided then that I would not work for *The Observer* again. I had broken one of the premier stories ever to come out of Northern Ireland and I felt it had been partially whipped away from me. My ego got to me.

Andy Wood had a government statement prepared for when the paper hit the stands late on Saturday night, which insisted that no one had been authorised to talk or negotiate with republicans, and went on to make an assertion which was to prove controversial – that in February 1993, a message had been passed to the government from the IRA leadership: 'It was to the effect that the conflict was over, but they needed advice as to the means of bringing it to a close. The government obviously had to take that message seriously.'

The confirmation of the existence of a back-channel left Patrick Mayhew with no choice but to face the press that Sunday. Camera crews from all over these islands rushed to Stormont

Castle to hear his explanations. This must have been the worst moment of his political career – he had been caught red-handed misleading me and was clearly flustered. During the press conference, Mayhew realised I wanted to ask a question just as Brian Rowan was also poised to put a question to him. Mayhew signalled he was ready to take my question, but I deferred to Rowan, which was the source of considerable hilarity amongst my colleagues as I wasn't known for deferring to anyone. As far as I was concerned, I had done my work. Fionnuala O'Connor said to the secretary of state at the press conference, 'I think we noticed you swallowing, and your syntax has gone to pieces several times.' David McKittrick of the *Independent* wrote of the event:

> The old Sir Patrick Mayhew was a big brusque character with a genial twinkle in his eye and a ready smile. Some in Belfast thought him perhaps a little patronising, but in general he was accepted as a man of rectitude and straight dealing, as indeed befits a former Attorney General. The new Sir Patrick Mayhew made his first appearance at Stormont last Sunday, pale, tense and unhappy. He stumbled through his explanations of why he had been in protracted contact with Sinn Féin and the IRA.

I felt this was my day. I had persevered for practically a year waiting for this moment. I had been derided by press officers in Downing Street and at Stormont, who had cast doubt about the credibility of what I was alleging.

On Monday 29 November, speaking in the House of Commons, Mayhew pledged to put a record of the government–

Sinn Féin contacts in the House of Commons library. His explanation for the contact was that a statement had come from Martin McGuinness, via a channel, effectively advising that the conflict was over. Sinn Féin immediately denied the allegation that Martin McGuinness had sent any correspondence of this nature to the British government. It emerged some years later that the statement to which Mayhew had been referring was actually the thoughts of three people, including the late Brendan Duddy and former priest Denis Bradley, who were used from time to time by the British government as a sounding board in its efforts to get a handle on the thinking of republicanism. It turned out that when Sinn Féin's record of the communications was set against the account given by the secretary of state, the latter was riddled with errors that Mayhew put down to typing and transmission mistakes. By December, it was being widely reported that Mayhew had offered to resign because of this; I learned recently that John Chilcot, permanent under-secretary of state at the NIO, had also offered to step down. Major refused to accept their resignations.

The following people were party to the secret contacts between Sinn Féin and the government: John Chilcot; his deputy, Quentin Thomas; Jonathan Stephens; John Deverell, MI5 agent; and David Cook, who was London based and worked for Quentin Thomas. They were the only five people, along with the secretary of state and the prime minister, who were across all the details of the contacts. In fact, when I exposed what had been going on, David Fell, the head of the Northern Ireland Civil Service rang me to tell me he was in the dark about the secret exchanges. Former Northern Ireland Security Minister Michael Mates later told me, 'To let local civil servants be involved would [have been] to test their unionism to the point of self-destruction.' The mantra of the day was 'for British eyes only'. That still rankles with some former senior Northern Ireland-based civil servants.

The most exposed and the most vulnerable of all that week in the House of Commons was Patrick Mayhew, who would have to defend the government's position, which by then had been shown to be suspect at best. One man in particular rode to his rescue – John Hume. Hume told me he went directly to the Labour Party leader, John Smith, and prevailed upon him not to table a motion of no confidence in Mayhew on the grounds that the Peace Process was more important and bigger than one man. Smith listened carefully and respectfully to Hume, and Mayhew survived. He would turn out to be Northern Ireland's longest-serving secretary of state, remaining in office until 1997.

***

Despite breaking this story, I had a reasonable working relationship with Patrick Mayhew during his tenure in Northern Ireland. On the day he was leaving we were called to Stormont Castle. The tall, patrician figure walked down the steps of the castle and got into the green Jaguar that was waiting for him. As the car drove away, I realised that I had just witnessed the thirteenth secretary of state of my working life departing Northern Ireland. But no sooner had the Jaguar pulled away than it reversed back. Mayhew stepped out of the car and walked straight up to me. He shook my hand and said, 'Goodbye, Eamonn, goodbye.' That was the last time I saw him.

He didn't shake hands with anybody else. That handshake signalled, in my opinion, a respect. I had 'got him', but he was man enough to accept that what I had done went with the turf.

I knew Mayhew's wife, Jean, a little while the family were in Northern Ireland. I liked what I heard about her: I was told she was known to take a genuine interest in people who were down at heel in London. I was aware too that she was planning to become an Anglican minister. A few years ago, Detta and I were having dinner in Café Conor on the Stranmillis Road when I spotted Chris Maccabe, a former senior NIO civil servant. He was in the company of an elderly lady whom I immediately recognised as Jean. I deduced from her reaction that she had also just recognised me. She immediately crossed the floor to us. I welcomed her back to Northern Ireland and introduced her to Detta. I was curious to know if she was still ministering in the Anglican Church. She told us that she was no longer doing so, having stepped back when her husband fell ill. I told Jean the story about Mayhew's farewell handshake with me on his last day in Northern Ireland. Before rejoining her host, she said, 'Eamonn ... it's an awful pity you and Patrick didn't get together after he left here. He used to say to me, "Eamonn knows – Eamonn knows what's going on."' I lament the fact that I didn't get a chance to have that postmortem with Mayhew years after his leaving Northern Ireland. Such is life.

***

I later learned that a delegation from the DUP, led by Ian Paisley, had held a face-to-face meeting with John Major at Downing Street on Friday 26 November. During the meeting, conscious of the secret letter that was in his pocket, McCrea challenged Major about reports of contact between the government and the IRA. The prime minister categorically dismissed these as rumours. Indeed, just a couple of weeks earlier, Major had told parliament that speaking to the IRA 'would turn my stomach'. McCrea had agreed not to share anything about the document until I had had it authenticated. I told him that if I was able to stand the story up, he would have his day in the sun when it was published – I would do everything I could to ensure he was acknowledged for his pivotal role in providing me with the document. He was 100 per cent true to his word. Sadly, William McCrea, who acted honourably, didn't get the attention he deserved.

On the Sunday the story broke in *The Observer*, Ian Paisley rang at two minutes to midnight and asked me to come to his house. Paisley didn't give interviews on Sunday unless the circumstances were exceptional. When I arrived at the Paisley home, just after midnight, he asked, 'Eamonn, why did I not know about these secret IRA talks when William McCrea knew?' I told him the background and explained that the reason he didn't know was because William had kept his word to me and had acted honourably. Paisley replied, 'Fair enough.'

When the whole furore around my exposure of the British government holding secrets talks with the IRA died down, a very senior English civil servant at the heart of the back-channel invited me for lunch. He shocked me when he disclosed that consideration had been given at one stage to try and 'co-opt' me. In the world of espionage this amounts to 'bringing someone on the inside' to either compromise them or control them. That would have been one hell of a scoop had I known it at the time.

Chapter Eight

The Good Friday Agreement

IRISH-AMERICANS MAKE UP CLOSE to 10 per cent of the US population, and among those thirty million are members of my family on my mother's side and on my father's side. Many of my family left this island in the second half of the 1800s, either during the Famine or after the Famine, while others emigrated in the first two decades of the 1900s. In many cases, they were not heard from again.

Historically, nationalists had a greater affinity with America. Unionists have been more cautious and sceptical about the US, feeling that Americans had too much empathy with republicans – especially during the Troubles. Despite this, it is an incontrovertible fact that Northern Ireland has contributed its fair share to the line of US presidents. During his 1995 trip to Northern Ireland, Bill Clinton acknowledged that one-third of all US presidents had ancestral roots in Northern Ireland.

The arrival of Clinton on the scene in 1993 opened up a new chapter in relations between Northern Ireland and the American administration. Without Clinton, I doubt if loyalists like Joe English and David Ervine, or republicans like Gerry Adams and Richard McAuley, or journalists like me, would have ever been allowed through the door of the White House. All my visits there took place during Clinton's presidency. Time changes everything. My father's father hadn't travelled more than fifteen miles from where he was born in South Armagh; I was regularly now dodging about the White House in Washington as the guest of Bill and Hillary Clinton. It was a far cry from the whitewashed house in which I was reared on the side of the hill in rural South Armagh.

I loved visiting the US. My first trip to America as a journalist took place in 1994, when I went as part of the press pack accompanying a delegation from Northern Ireland. During that visit, Gerry Adams and Ken Maginnis, the Ulster Unionist MP, were both guests on *Larry King Live*. After the broadcast, Adams came out of the studio to speak to members of the press. I noticed that he was covering his crotch with a newspaper. I later asked what was this all about. His aide Richard McAuley explained to me that while Adams was larking about in the green room before going on set, his zip went, with the result that he did his interview with his fly in distress. In the course of exchanges on air, Ken Maginnis produced a copy of *The Sunday Times* in which there was a story that was not complimentary to Gerry Adams, a story that Adams hadn't seen. He asked Maginnis to pass the paper to him – he held on to it and it proved useful when he was speaking to the press afterwards to shield his embarrassment.

I returned to the US in May 1995 for an economic conference in Washington, the aim of which was to promote Northern Ireland as a location for inward investment. Most of the Northern Ireland political parties were represented at that conference. It was a wonderful occasion when loyalists, republicans, nationalists and unionists came together like a family at every level.

The Sheraton Hotel was the venue for the conference. It was there that a meeting between Patrick Mayhew and Gerry Adams took place. That encounter happened on the sixth floor in Room 666. I still have not worked out whether Adams or Mayhew gained more from the talks that took place in a room bearing that number. Neither Mayhew nor any member of his government had met anyone from Sinn Féin up to that point, but the Americans put pressure on the secretary of state and the British to meet Adams since they were both under the same roof at the conference. The arrangements for that particular meeting were not simple. For Sinn Féin, they were in the hands of Richard McAuley. The British Embassy team was keen to move the meeting away from the Sheraton to another venue because of the large media presence in the hotel. According to McAuley, he had to put pressure on Mayhew's advisors – British Ambassador Robin Renwick and his colleague Peter Westmacott – to make it clear to them that Sinn Féin was not moving. Incidentally, Peter Westmacott's cousin, Captain Richard Westmacott, had been shot dead in an IRA M50 machine-gun attack in May 1980 when operating on the Antrim Road in North Belfast. It was a killing that I had always remembered, and during this visit I had a chance to talk to Captain Westmacott's cousin about it.

Richard McAuley painted a picture for me of what happened in the room before Adams and Mayhew arrived. McAuley left to get Adams, and a colleague, Mick Conlon, remained behind with the English diplomats. McAuley told me, 'Mick said to me as I exited, "I'm beginning to feel a bit like a hostage." The English guys all laughed.' When I asked why he left his man in the room with Mayhew's team, McAuley told me, 'It was instinctive and automatic to do so. I thought it was better keeping one of our people in the room. It is something you do on the spur of the moment.' I doubted this – those boys leave nothing to chance. While McAuley was out of the room, Conlon and Renwick struck up a conversation and discovered they both had a passion for fly fishing. Conlon was talking up fly fishing in Donegal, while Renwick said that Alaska was the best place in the world for casting a fly. As the conversation broke up, the Sinn Féin man said to Renwick, 'Well, maybe some time we could share a fly in Alaska.'

When Adams and Mayhew arrived and the introductions had taken place, the meeting got under way. Mayhew – who, according to McAuley, seemed nervous – explained at the outset of the meeting that he would be referring to speaking notes. He said he needed to use them to make sure that he got all his points across. Sinn Féin then presented Mayhew with a position document. According to McAuley, a civilised discussion took place between Mayhew and Adams. McAuley recalled, 'We saw it as an opportunity to deal with Mayhew at a personal level. Gerry said to the guy, "What I want to persuade you of is that we are serious. We have a lot invested in this."' He added, 'The idea was, if we can plant a seed then we could talk politics later. We wanted to plant a seed that hopefully later, having reflected upon it, Patrick Mayhew would realise this was an opportunity to do business with republicans. The guy had never talked to a republican before. One phrase comes to mind when I think back. Adams said, "You and I are political enemies, coming to this situation from very different positions. It would be easy to lock horns, but that is not what we need."' McAuley told me, 'Mayhew was cool, courteous and intelligent,' adding, 'there were one or two occasions when it was clear our positions were different'.

When Adams emerged at the end of the meeting, there was pandemonium in the corridors of the Sheraton Hotel. There were dozens and dozens of camerapeople, sound recordists and reporters waiting for him. We were all corralled in a narrow corridor. My microphone was attached to my tape recorder by a rather short cable, and I quickly realised that it was going to be impossible to catch what Adams was saying with sufficiently good quality. I decided to pass my tape recorder and my microphone, complete with the Downtown flag, through a sea of journalists' hands and camerapeople. It ended up with a big man who was standing guard beside Adams. The guard, at a loss as to what to do, handed the microphone to the Sinn Féin president. Gerry Adams hosted his entire press conference with my microphone in his hand, flying Downtown Radio's flag. Even in Washington, over 3,000 miles away, I could hear some of those BBC news editors back in Belfast going ballistic, screaming at the screen, 'There is that bastard Mallie's microphone stuck in our shots.'

Following the Adams press conference, we had been invited to the White House. The norm was that we would have an opportunity at some stage to meet the president and his wife. This time was no exception. I met him and had my photograph taken with him. By this time, he must have been sick looking at me. On this occasion, my name and the names of my fellow political correspondents from Ireland, North and South, were forwarded to the White House by the Irish ambassador of that time, Seán Ó hUiginn. Everyone given access to the White House as a visitor is schooled on how to behave by whomever invited them. People are asked not to be overfamiliar with the president or his wife, but there is always one who violates the protocol. At times, I might have been that person!

I decided I would try to bring my tape recorder with me into the White House reception during that trip in 1995, just on the off chance I might get an opportunity to fire a question at the president. I am still baffled as to how I got away with it. My goal was to get an on-the-hoof interview. The Clintons were 'working the rope' when I noticed that Gerry Burns – chief executive of Fermanagh District Council – was in line to meet them shortly. I slipped over to Gerry and warned him that I was going to try to get a few words with Clinton. Just when the president was about to shake hands with Gerry, he said to him, 'Mr President, this is a decent lad from home. He's a reporter, maybe you'll have a word with him?'

'Mr President,' I said, 'there is a lot of speculation back home that you intend to visit Northern Ireland. Is there any truth in that?' Clinton replied, 'We are working on a schedule and if we can get it together, we'll be there.'

Scoop! My only interest now was in getting my story back to my news desk in Downtown Radio. One of the killers about reporting from the US is the time difference. We were so many hours behind that it was hard to connect with the news bulletins back home. However, this was definitely a lead story. It was the first time that we had heard from the horse's mouth that the president of the United States intended to visit Northern Ireland. Eventually, I managed to dispatch the Clinton interview as well as the audio from Gerry Adams' press conference after his meeting with Mayhew. In the aftermath of all the main television bulletins, I received a 'herogram' from my news editor, telling me how excited everyone at Downtown Radio was because the company flag had been seen on every outlet throughout the United Kingdom. To this day, no one has ever asked me, 'Eamonn, how did you get that exclusive interview with President Clinton?' My scoop was ignored. It's all about the money in commercial companies.

When the international economic conference finished in the Sheraton Hotel in 1995, we had a night of entertainment that ran well into the early hours of the morning. David Fell, the head of the Civil Service in Northern Ireland, played the piano and his wife, Sandra, charmed us with her mellifluous voice. The SDLP's Seamus Mallon and Joe Hendron, joined by the UUP's Roy Beggs, held court practically the whole night, singing the best of Irish songs. Another star that particular evening was Hughie Smyth of the PUP. That was an evening to remember: when nationalists and unionists came together away from home. We could only dream that there would be more nights like this.

It is easy to forget the access that people from Northern Ireland had to the White House during Clinton's tenure. Not only elected members of political parties met the president in his own home, but their associates from republican and loyalist organisations, from working-class areas, found themselves in the Oval Office, in conversation with the president and having their photograph taken with him. Businessmen from all around the world would pay millions of dollars to get into that Oval Office to have their photographs taken with the president. That is what was so rare about Clinton. He was so smart. He knew perfectly well with whom he was dealing from both communities but, like John Hume, he was a big-picture man who was prepared to take chances to win the big prize – peace. Joe English was among the loyalists who visited the Oval Office and met Clinton. He told my colleague Deric Henderson afterwards of the pleasure he had derived from wearing his red-and-black Crusaders FC tie on that occasion.

Anywhere President Clinton went, there was sure to be fun. We were outside the Europa Hotel in Belfast one day when he was about to emerge. The crowd-control barriers were in place and we, as journalists and camera people, had all assembled. Practically every woman around the city had heard that Clinton was in the Europa and a crowd had now formed behind us. As the president emerged through the front door, I turned to one of the women and said, 'One question: what do you want to ask him?' That woman declined to answer, but up stepped her friend who said, 'What night are you free?' That was the type of reaction President Clinton inspired. I have not seen or known anyone with his charisma.

On another visit to Northern Ireland, Clinton was going to the Clinton Centre, which is at the site of the 1987 Remembrance Day bombing in Enniskillen. It was a hot day and I was desperately chasing around the house looking for a pair of sunglasses. I couldn't find my own, but I found a neon-blue pair that belonged to Michael. I stuck them on and hurtled up the motorway, slightly late starting out. On arrival at the Clinton Centre, Gerry Burns, the chief executive of the council, spotted photographer John Harrison and me outside and took us into the courtyard at the back. He told us that the president's car would be coming straight into the yard. When Clinton jumped out of the car, he came straight over to me and said, 'Let me see your shades.' I handed them to him and he lifted them to his face. His press aide, Jennifer Palmieri, said, 'No, Mr President; no, Mr President', but it was too late. John Harrison had captured on camera President Clinton with my child's neon-blue sunglasses inches away from his eyes. That was Clinton. He was full of devilment. You just wouldn't know what he was going to do next. He lit up every room.

On one trip to Belfast, Clinton visited Parliament Buildings. All the Assembly members had gathered in the Great Hall to meet him. He worked the hall skilfully as always and, as is normal in situations like that, when the guest leaves, the media are anxious to hear what the visitor had said or wanted to know about his or her hosts. Barry McElduff, Sinn Féin MLA for West Tyrone, was asked, 'What did President Clinton say to you, Barry?' Quick as a flash, he replied, 'He asked me, "Did the bumper go at the Bingo the other night in Ardboe?"'

***

The depth of interest that Clinton took in the affairs of Northern Ireland was disproportionate to that taken by any of his predecessors. Not even the Kennedys engaged as much with Ireland.

It was during his campaign for the presidency that he started to familiarise himself with Irish-American affairs, encouraged by people like Niall O'Dowd, the editor of the *Irish Voice*, the leading Irish paper in America. Clinton's early involvement in Irish affairs would have far-reaching implications for the faltering search for peace, which would culminate in the loyalist and republican ceasefires, followed by the negotiations chaired by US Senator George Mitchell in 1998.

During an economic crisis in the mid-1960s, Harold Wilson famously said, 'A week is a long time in politics.' I can honestly say that the final four days of the negotiations that would lead to the Good Friday Agreement in April 1998 felt like an eternity.

Up until this point, the prospect of an end to all political violence and the creation of a local power-sharing administration at Parliament Buildings had appeared remote, despite the 1994 IRA and loyalist ceasefires. But Labour had come into power in the UK in spring 1997, and Prime Minister Tony Blair was determined to achieve what many prime ministers before him had failed to do: secure an end to all violence in Northern Ireland and establish permanent political structures.

Five months after his 1997 landslide election victory, Tony Blair shook hands with Sinn Féin President Gerry Adams. Blair was the first prime minister to take a Sinn Féin hand since David Lloyd George in the 1920s. The foundations had by now been well laid for a rapprochement between the Labour government and republicans. Labour's shadow spokesperson on Northern Ireland, Mo Mowlam, told the BBCNI that her party would accept Sinn Féin at the talks table conditional on there being no violence for six weeks – the IRA ceasefire had ended in June 1996. The meeting became possible when the IRA restored its ceasefire in July 1997.

We were briefed very specifically at the time that the handshake had taken place deliberately at Stormont and not in Downing Street. Apart from Gerry Adams, also attending that meeting with Blair were Martin McGuinness, Pat Doherty and Siobhán O'Hanlon. The talks in Castle Buildings at Stormont, which culminated in the Good Friday Agreement, staggered along week after week with little real progress and paranoia was a common factor among all the parties involved in the meetings, each deeply suspicious of being wrong-footed. Seamus Mallon expressed his worry to Tony Blair that his party might 'get gobbled up by Sinn Féin'.

On 23 March 1998, best friends Philip Allen, a Protestant, and Damien Trainor, a Catholic, were shot dead by the Loyalist Volunteer Force (LVF) in the Railway Bar in Poyntzpass in County Armagh. Their killings came against a backdrop of ongoing sterile political wrangling. US Senator George Mitchell was appointed by Bill Clinton to chair the negotiations for a peace deal. He had not yet set the deadline of 9 April for the end of negotiations, despite the fact that the SDLP had previously been pressing him to name a definitive date. In reply to particular assertions by Seamus Mallon on this matter, Senator Mitchell said, 'I am Humpty Dumpty and can only jump once ...' He was not ruling a deadline out but was stressing the importance of timing and questioning the evidence of alignment or adjustment across the thinking of the parties.

The morning after the double killing in Poyntzpass, the deputy leader of the SDLP advised Mark Durkan that he was heading to the village with the expectation that David Trimble might also be there. Durkan told me, 'Around the Talks table there was a sombre but palpable sense of purpose as the parties present affirmed the need to show the primacy of dialogue over violence. I said that the warm stories of Philip and Damien's special friendship could be a parable for the sort of society that we might create if we could reach agreement.' Durkan's brain had by now gone into overdrive. He told me, 'Lunchtime's

TV news carried the pictures of Seamus and David together in Poyntzpass. I was struck by the image of leaders from two different traditions symbolically binding the wounds of the community. My mind moved to an idea of joint First Ministers being jointly elected by the Assembly as a way of answering some of the conundrums and criticisms attaching to our D'Hondt proposals.' Victor D'Hondt, a Belgian lawyer and jurist in civil law, created a way of sharing out seats in the wake of elections. This method was used in the Northern Ireland Assembly to distribute ministerial seats among parties based on their electoral performances. Clearly, Senator Mitchell was reading a room in a more buoyant mood – and on 25 March, he set 9 April as the deadline for the negotiations. The names Allen and Trainor ought to be inextricably identified forever with what was a political miracle, 'The Good Friday Agreement'. They, like so many others, paid the ultimate price – death – for our peace.

On the night of Monday 6 April, with only a few days to go until the deadline, the Irish government tossed a political grenade into the Ulster Unionist camp in the form of a paper which prescribed multiple cross-border bodies. It became known as 'the Mitchell document'. I am told that George Mitchell contemplated asking Kelly Currie, his communications director, to come out to tell me that he wanted it to be made known that the document was not of his making but had been foisted upon him by the two governments for distribution to the parties on Monday night. Mitchell had known instantly that it would not be acceptable to the unionists. He considered it too pro-nationalist because of its emphasis on a strong all-Ireland dimension. In an account of the negotiations written by Tony

Blair's chief advisor, John Holmes, marked 'confidential', but which I have read, Holmes states that he realised the Mitchell document had pushed the unionists over the edge because it had not been an agreed work. The big fear was that David Trimble and his team might walk without dramatic changes to what unionists viewed as Dublin's unreasonably 'green' demands.

Tony Blair's advisors urged him to come to Northern Ireland to try to save the faltering negotiations on Tuesday 7 April. When the prime minister spoke at Hillsborough Castle that Tuesday afternoon, he said, 'A day like today is not a day for soundbites, really. But I feel the hand of history upon our shoulders. I really do.' I was not alone in thinking this comment could end up rendering him a hostage to fortune. According to his director of communications, Alastair Campbell, he and the PM's principal private secretary, John Holmes, were baffled by the tone struck by their boss. When I recently pressed Blair on that now-famous remark and asked him what prompted it, he said, 'I don't know. It literally came into my head at the time. You laughed at me; so did my entire staff and I laughed at myself actually afterwards. I don't know how ever that happened.'

Early on the morning of Monday 6 April, Taoiseach Bertie Ahern's mother had died in Dublin. I am reminded here of a quote from Harold Macmillan, who, when asked what the greatest challenge was for a statesman, replied, 'Events, dear boy, events.' Ahern's waking of his mother was interrupted on the Tuesday night by both Tony Blair and George Mitchell informing him of the urgent need for radical change to his Department of Foreign Affairs' document that was driving unionists batty. Ulster Unionist MP John Taylor dismissed Blair's optimism in an interview with me outside Castle Buildings, in which he said of the Dublin document, 'I wouldn't touch it with a 40-foot barge pole.' Ahern was left with no choice but to head for Hillsborough Castle for a meeting with Blair at the crack of dawn on Wednesday morning to calm nerves in British and unionist camps. Ulster Unionist Reg Empey told me, 'Had Bertie not come back from waking his mother we were down the tubes. If he hadn't come back to manage and control the Department of Foreign Affairs [blamed by the unionists for writing the document] we were out the door. We felt this was a backdoor to a Council of Ireland. There would have been bodies operating with executive powers throughout the island.' It had been talk of a Council of Ireland meeting following the 1973 Sunningdale Agreement that resulted in Ian Paisley torpedoing the 1974 power-sharing executive. Gradually, the negotiations settled down in the wake of Mrs Ahern's funeral, helped by the taoiseach taking the scalpel to many of the cross-border bodies that the unionists found offensive.

I took it upon myself to extend condolences to the taoiseach on the death of his mother and to acknowledge his commitment to the Peace Process outside Castle Buildings on behalf of the assembled press. I always believe in leading from the front when I think I should stand up and be counted. Ahern graciously acknowledged my comments. I was taken aback when a TV correspondent from the Republic of Ireland took me to task for doing what I felt was the decent thing in the circumstances.

Journalists like me were now living on scraps of information gleaned from endless press conferences and calls to well-placed contacts in the parties. I wasn't getting much sleep, having to be on the floorboards as early as 6 a.m. daily to do interviews for London TV and radio programmes. Northern Ireland was hot right then, with Tony Blair based here during the negotiations, groping his way through the process with his 'hand of history' desperately trying to avoid the sword of Damocles.

***

At the very heart of the Good Friday Agreement were the constants that had been promoted by John Hume for years – three sets of relationships: within Northern Ireland; between North and South; and between Britain and the Republic of Ireland. The SDLP leader was emphatic about consent being necessary for any change to the status of Northern Ireland, and he urged that any political settlement in Northern Ireland should be subject to referendums in both parts of the island of Ireland. His philosophy was that 'the double minority problem could be resolved with a double majority solution'.

Sinn Féin did not engage in talks about Strand One – a power-sharing executive in Northern Ireland, in what they saw as a partitioned State – until the final week of the negotiations. When I asked Mitchel McLaughlin about this and what had changed, he explained that the right to self-determination – first expressed in Peter Brooke's seminal speech in which he stated, 'the British government has no selfish strategic or economic interest in Northern Ireland' and reinforced in the Downing Street Declaration of 1993 – had become a fixed element of any settlement.

The negotiations stumbled from one crisis to the next, triggered by genuine concerns and paranoia in all the parties.

Ulster Unionists were terrified of ending up in government with Sinn Féin before the whole issue of decommissioning was resolved, or before republicans had shown a willingness to support policing and much more. Ahern dreaded conceding Articles 2 and 3 of the Irish Constitution, which claimed jurisdiction over Northern Ireland, concerned that the UUP might return asking for further concessions. Seamus Mallon told Blair of his party's concerns of 'being gobbled up' by Sinn Féin. John Holmes says in his document, 'We attached importance to making explicit the principle of "mutually assured destruction", whereby all the new institutions were mutually interdependent and could not function without each other.' Sinn Féin made it clear to Tony Blair days before the agreement on April 10 that they needed guarantees on the early release of republican prisoners for their buy-in to any agreement.

So, what were the tools used by the British and Irish governments in dealing with the parties to overcome the plethora of difficulties? One critical measure used was 'constructive ambiguity' – or, as Mark Durkan described it, 'complete ambiguity'. This is the deliberate use of ambiguous language on a sensitive issue in order to advance a political plan. A fudge is a more honest way of putting it. This is a common tactic in political negotiations going back to Henry Kissinger's time. Tony Blair was a proponent of this to get over hurdles. To advance the talks the prime ministers and their negotiating teams had to be selective in what they let rival parties know. As Patrick Mayhew put it, 'It is all about keeping the bicycle upright and moving forward.'

Secret 'comfort' or 'side' letters were used when necessary. Towards the end of that week, David Trimble was facing a rebellion in his ranks over the question of entering a Stormont administration before the IRA had started 'decommissioning'. Holmes' document states that after meeting David Trimble, John Taylor, Reg Empey, Ken Maginnis and Jeffrey Donaldson, 'we concocted a letter to Trimble making clear that, if after 6 months of the Assembly the present rules to promote non-violent methods had proved ineffective, we would support changing the rules to give them teeth'.

Blair's office went further. It enlisted President Clinton's help, asking him to ring Trimble directly. Even Trimble fell for Clinton's charms. Soon, the word was filtering through to journalists from UUP members in hushed tones that the president had been on the phone to the party leader! Trimble now had the British government's 'concocted' letter in his pocket plus a conversation with Bill Clinton. This released some of the pus from the unionist boil.

***

In the early hours of the morning of Friday 10 April, perhaps at half two or three o'clock, I spotted something extraordinary through bleary eyes. From my position beyond the gates at Castle Buildings, I could just about see through the windows of where the talks were taking place. One of the longest-serving members of the SDLP, Bríd Rodgers, was hugging and kissing Seamus Mallon. Did this mean white smoke? Had the parties reached an agreement? More hugging took place, involving Rodgers and her colleagues Tommy Gallagher and Donovan McClelland. I learned later that the UUP had agreed with the SDLP on Strand One, the internal structures for an executive at

Parliament Buildings, in the wake of Strand Two being settled between them and Dublin. Seamus Mallon had returned to his party's office to apprise them of this breakthrough, which had sparked all the hugging and bonhomie in the SDLP. Tony Blair had also unilaterally decided that there would be six seats for each constituency in future Assembly elections, thereby allowing greater opportunities for the smaller parties to play a fuller role in the administration. Even without knowing any of these details, my colleagues and I were now wide awake, fired up by the prospect of an official announcement in the coming hours.

Northern Ireland comedian Jimmy Cricket's famous catch-phrase was 'and there's more', and there was another develop-ment at around 5.30 a.m. Sinn Féin made a tactical intervention in sending Mitchel McLaughlin out to speak to the media. Kenny Rogers' famous song 'The Gambler' says, 'You've got to know when to hold 'em, know when to fold 'em ... There'll be time enough for countin' when the dealin's done.' Sinn Féin wasn't finished dealing. A raft of issues was yet to be resolved for the republican family as a whole, but particularly for the families of prisoners throughout the islands. These families were critical to the Sinn Féin leadership in shoring them up electorally. Mitchel McLaughlin told me, 'We didn't need an agreement in principle; we needed specifics to bring back to the prisoners and to their families.'

Sinn Féin also had other fish to fry: a deal on so-called 'escapees subject to arrest' or so-called on-the-runs. A letter on this issue was advanced to Sinn Féin by Mo Mowlam in the dying days of the negotiations. Sinn Féin wanted their prisoners out in one year but settled for two. David Ervine of the PUP advised

Sinn Féin's Gerry Kelly that 'the people will not wear prisoner release in one year'.

Gradually, all the pieces of the jigsaw were falling into place. John Holmes writes that suddenly, at about 4.30 p.m., 'rumours reached us that following the prime minister's letter and Clinton's call, Trimble had taken renewed heart and called a vote, which he had narrowly won. This seemed to be too good to be true, but Trimble quickly rang to confirm that the way was now clear for the plenary to be held and Mitchell arranged it for 5 o'clock.' The vote was swift. All said yes except Adams, who according to Holmes was 'very positive' about the text 'but would have to consult his Annual Conference first'. Holmes said, 'Trimble said he would have to consult his Executive Committee and full Executive Council but was voting yes anyhow. There was no applause when sufficient consensus was achieved – just a stunned silence.'

Up until this point, I had always thought David Trimble would be a mere footnote in history. Happily, he proved me wrong. Ultimately, Trimble concluded Sinn Féin must be part of any political solution and that is what came to pass through his creativity and doggedness. Tony Blair's naysayers – including me – now had to accept that 'the hand of history' was indeed on our shoulders.

* * *

Like so much else about the making of the Belfast/Good Friday Agreement, the very naming of it was made up on the hoof. It was Dublin civil servant Rory Montgomery, born in Northern Ireland, who recommended that the agreement reached on

Good Friday in 1998 should be called 'The Belfast Agreement'. He contended such an appellation would be in line with the European Union (EU) norm of naming accords/treaties after the city in which they were signed, such as the Maastricht Treaty, the Treaty of Rome and The Hague Convention.

Then taoiseach, and one of the architects of the agreement, Bertie Ahern pushed back against his own civil servant's argument for calling the deal 'The Belfast Agreement'. Despite this, the Irish government in official documents dealing with changes to the Irish Constitution agreed in Castle Buildings did not mention the term 'Good Friday Agreement'. Former SDLP leader Mark Durkan opines that the latter term possibly emerged in the vernacular as a 'constitutional colloquialism', because of the use of the word 'Good' in the Good Friday Agreement. I am told the last thing nationalists wanted was for it to be called 'The Stormont Agreement'.

Undoubtedly, George Mitchell was the ballast that gave the Stormont negotiations weight and an international focus. Mitchell's first posting to Northern Ireland had been in 1995, when Clinton had made him US special envoy. Initially, he had led an international body to review options for the decommissioning of paramilitary arms that would ultimately produce the ground rules on which future negotiations would be based. These became known as the Mitchell Principles. He had experience as the majority leader in the Senate on Capitol Hill and was also a judge. I am told he was keen to be the US secretary of state but was given a consolation prize of coming to Northern Ireland to try to undo the political deadlock. His stature and gravitas brought reality to the Stormont negotiations, and I think he is one of the most skilful communicators I have ever come across. I found it impossible to land a punch any time I interviewed him.

It has been suggested to me that the senator had considered walking away several times during much of the inertia in the process. He had his own affairs at home to deal with, which meant dividing his time between Northern Ireland and America, which was proving challenging. I gather there came a point when the possibility of having to find an alternative chairman was coming into focus in the rearview mirror.

Martha Pope, who was chief advisor to Mitchell during the Good Friday negotiations, shared some facts with me about the anvil upon which the agreement was forged. Pope told me, 'It always had to be the parties and the governments to do the deal. Senator Mitchell didn't have the power or the tools nor the history for the talks and negotiations when it came to cutting the deal. When Blair and Ahern arrived, we were shuffled into oblivion. We were nowhere. We were invisible. Mitchell met the parties, but he didn't negotiate. The parties weren't aware at the time how irrelevant we had become.'

Someone whose opinion I trust without reservation held the view that Mitchell was always more sympathetic to the difficulties facing unionism than to those of republicanism, but the biggest row during the week of the Good Friday Agreement talks was not between Mitchell and republicans, but between Mitchell and SDLP deputy leader Seamus Mallon. Mitchell was not known to be a contrarian. At no point was that ever suggested to me by either Martha Pope or Kelly Currie, who worked with him during the negotiations for the agreement. There are many, however, who were very ready to acknowledge that Mallon was no wilting violet and didn't mind engaging in the rough and tumble of life on the football field or in his public life of politics. I know that is true because I felt the sharp edge of his tongue on a number of occasions. According to Mark Durkan, the SDLP's political guru, a chasm opened up between Mitchell and Mallon on the question of issues like policing. The former Newry–Armagh MP argued policing had to be part of any agreement and he made this very clear, face to face with Mitchell. His contention was other matters such as policing under talks' rules were permissible. He thought that Mitchell had conceded this point, but when nothing happened either inside the talks chamber or outside, he thought the senator said something that was 'misleading'. I am told that at one stage, Mallon threatened to have his own note-taker present during future meetings with Mitchell. According to Durkan, had talks co-chairman, former Finnish Prime Minister Harri Holkeri, not intervened during a meeting, inviting Mallon to his room at that point, potentially it would have been 'a fairly intemperate exchange'.

During the GFA25 Conference at Queen's University, George Mitchell revisited his exchanges with Seamus Mallon in conversation with Durkan. He told him, 'Whenever Seamus was arguing with me, I used to think I had got something wrong myself.' Clearly, Mallon had left a mark of his size 9–10 GAA boot on the talks chairman's memory.

Mitchell's relationship with other politicians at the talks was not so fraught. Dawn Purvis of the PUP said that in a conversation with her party leader, David Ervine, Mitchell gave him to understand he did not believe there would be a deal. Ervine replied, 'I'll bet you a bottle of champagne we'll get a deal.' Mitchell replied, 'If we get a deal I'll buy you a case of champagne.' Dawn Purvis assures me that the champagne that subsequently arrived 'was not wasted'.

From my earliest experiences dealing with politicians here, I realised that one of the great negatives bedevilling them is paranoia. This mistrust of each other is common to all political parties, but unionists were especially suspicious of any Dublin involvement. They stuck *caveat emptor* on all communications with Europe and America. Their antipathy towards and suspicion of Americans surfaced very quickly during the peace negotiations, with younger unionists especially displaying gratuitous disrespect for George Mitchell and his team. Pope spoke to me of her 'disgust' at how awful their behaviour was.

However, she summed up her overall experience thus: 'We were just hugely lucky to get to do it. You are measured as a person in terms of your contribution to others. The time I spent in my life improving my own doesn't matter. It's the contribution to others. It's a privilege if it falls in your lap. For me the most powerful moment was when Mitchell was going around the room for the vote. It was just powerful. This was it. There was solemnity. The fix was in. The dignity and power of the occasion was palpable.'

Nelson Mandela once said, 'If you want to make peace with your enemy, you have to work with your enemy. Then he becomes your partner.' Such wise words were so apt for precisely what happened during the 1998 Good Friday negotiations.

I felt privileged to have been a witness to a once-in-a-lifetime political miracle, put better by Seamus Heaney, who wrote in the wake of Nelson Mandela's release from prison:

History says, don't hope
On this side of the grave.
But then, once in a lifetime
The longed-for tidal wave
Of justice can rise up,
And hope and history rhyme.

Chapter Nine

Unique Individuals

I OFTEN TELL MY friends that the two most obstinate and inflexible people I encountered in my working life were Margaret Thatcher and Charles J. Haughey. No one else's opinion seemed to matter to either of them – they had an extraordinary capacity to ignore reporters' questions, and to stick stubbornly to their own message, even if that meant giving the same answer over and over again. There is an irony attaching to this criticism – both Thatcher and Haughey fascinated me. I was dealing with two people who seemed to me to be concerned only with serving their own self-interests. They resented being held to account, despite being answerable to electorates.

On one occasion, in the run-up to a general election in the Republic of Ireland, I was at a very eventful press conference, during which journalist Vincent Browne interrogated Haughey about his personal finances. At the end of the press conference, I approached Haughey and asked for a one-to-one interview. He reluctantly agreed and, as we made our way to a quiet corner, he said, 'I am f–king sick' – or it might have been 'bucking sick' – 'of English journalists asking me questions about Northern Ireland. There are no votes for me in the North.' It appeared that he was putting me in the same bracket as the English journalists – but, in fairness, he did a good interview with me.

His gatekeeper and director of communications was a character called P.J. Mara. Mara was a larger-than-life individual with whom I had a good working relationship. When I appeared at any press conference, his refrain was 'No cheeky questions from you, you wee Northern f–ker, you.'

During some research for a book that I was writing with my colleague David McKittrick in the mid-1990s, I learned that Charles Haughey had helped to kick-start the Peace Process. Historians have not given him much credit for this. When I phoned his home to ask if he would be happy to talk to me about his role, he agreed to see me. I had read all about Haughey's wealth and his opulent lifestyle. Many questions had been asked down the years about how he could afford to live in his Abbeville mansion in Kinsealy, North Dublin, and afford his Charvet shirts from Paris. Several books have been written about Haughey and his wealth. However, probing Haughey's overt wealth was not my remit – it was his involvement in efforts to break the political deadlock that interested me.

There was no getting away from the opulence and the grandeur of the home in which Haughey lived. It was idyllic – a mansion set in a large tract of land with mature trees dotted across the sweeping lawns at the front of the house. When I arrived and pressed the doorbell, I looked out across the lush lawns and saw a cock pheasant and a number of hens beneath a huge tree, enjoying the balmy weather. When Haughey opened the door, I was struck firstly by how small he was and secondly by his casual dress. Drawing his attention to the scene beneath the tree, I sensed a little light came on. 'Ah,' he said, 'there he is over there, the cock strutting among the hens.' I wondered whether Haughey was revealing something of his own personality in his admiration for that pheasant and his female companions?

When I entered the atrium, the first thing I spotted was a painting by Cork artist Patrick Hennessy hanging to my left. I am familiar with his work and I remarked, 'I like that Hennessy. That's a good Hennessy.' I added, 'I see you have the lover on the other wall.' Haughey looked surprised and said, 'Oh – I didn't think you knew anything about this stuff.' Hennessy was a very distinguished painter in the realist tradition. He was homosexual and his lover was another artist, Harry Robertson Craig, whose work also hung in Haughey's hall. Both artists spent a lot of time together in Tangier.

Haughey then told me an interesting story about the Hennessy painting, filling me in firstly on how he came to have it. He had been in Leo Smith's gallery in Dublin some years earlier and had seen the Hennessy painting of a white horse drinking at a sunlit pool. He was particularly pleased to learn why the artist had put a moon in the top left-hand corner of the canvas. It was to indicate when he painted the work: 1969, the year man landed on the moon.

The Hennessy work was delivered to the Haughey home in due course. The morning after the painting was hung, Haughey was admiring it but – when he looked closely – he realised that it hadn't been signed by the artist. He asked his secretary to phone Leo Smith. They arranged that Smith would get in touch the next time Hennessy was in town; Haughey's secretary, Mairéad, suggested that she could send the State car to bring him to the house to sign the painting. Eventually, Haughey got word that Hennessy was in town and had time to drop out to

Abbeville. The car was dispatched so that he would arrive in time for supper. It was de rigueur in the Haughey pile for the butler to whet the guests' appetite with a little Veuve Clicquot champagne ahead of the meal in the Malton Room. Haughey and his new friend ate well and became seriously acquainted with champagne, drinking late into the night. Hennessy left Haughey on a high, clearly delighted by the hospitality afforded him. As Haughey strolled about the house the next morning, admiring his fine works of art and the many portraits of himself, he discovered that the Hennessy painting of the white horse at the sunlit pool still hadn't been signed by the artist. That was work for another day.

I can't begin to tell you how my day took off as a result of that initial encounter in Haughey's vestibule. I had gone to Abbeville in the hope of doing some serious research about his involvement in the initial efforts to put a Peace Process in place. In fact, we didn't exchange one single word about it. Art, literature, beekeeping, Brehon law and all the rest took over. We recited poetry; we exchanged views. During my encounter with Haughey, at no point did his wife, Maureen, join us in our conversations. I think in my three visits to Abbeville, I only saw her once.

I wasn't entirely surprised that in Haughey I found a remarkably resourceful, educated and well-read individual. He had a challenging mind and was someone who did not let the dog get away with his bone, interrogating every remark I uttered. He took me through the house into his private bar, created to his own design, taking great pride in telling me that the optics came from a bombed-out pub in Belfast. He had commissioned Tom Ryan, the former president of the Royal

Hibernian Academy, and fellow artist Muriel Brandt to make a huge painting of his local hunt, which hung on the main wall of the bar. Detta remarked – after she'd accompanied me on a subsequent visit – that she had counted close to a dozen portraits of Haughey dotted all over the house. It was abundantly clear that he loved art and he loved literature. In one of the upstairs rooms, I spotted a large Basil Blackshaw fighting-cock painting, around which a flotilla of nymphs danced on a surrounding mount.

We had lunch in the Malton Room. What a room! It was like something from Downton Abbey. It had a wonderful library feeling, with a suite of Malton drawings of old Dublin hanging from the picture rails. The room represented style and taste. During the meal, Haughey discussed poetry with me at length, giving preference to Patrick Kavanagh over Seamus Heaney. He argued that he had a greater affinity with Kavanagh's rawness and ruralism, rather than with Heaney, and told me an anecdote about Kavanagh, whom he had known and liked.

The inspiration for Kavanagh's famous poem about unrequited love, 'Raglan Road', was his muse, Hilda Moriarty, a young woman from Kerry who was studying to be a doctor in Dublin. She lived near Kavanagh in Ballsbridge. Kavanagh folklore has it that he once cycled the whole way to Kerry to visit Moriarty's home, but when he arrived she told him, 'Get on your bike, Paddy, and cycle back to Dublin.' Moriarty later married the distinguished Fianna Fáil Minister for Education Donogh O'Malley, a visionary who introduced free education for all children up to Intermediate Certificate level, as well as granting free bus passes for children in rural areas. O'Malley died at forty-seven.

Haughey clearly admired both O'Malley and Moriarty. He told me that down through the years, at the tea table and around the dinner table, he had regaled his children with stories about Kavanagh, and talked especially about 'Raglan Road' and the beautiful Hilda Moriarty. He told me how he had described her in detail: her exquisite beauty and her gorgeous dark hair. As an EU function in Dublin Castle approached, it occurred to Haughey that Hilda O'Malley had been somewhat overlooked since the passing of her husband. He decided to invite her to sit at his family table at the banquet. He told his family again about Kavanagh's muse with her long, dark hair. Come the night of the event, Haughey told me there was an air of great anticipation at their table among his family who had heard so much about this *spéirbhean* (beautiful woman) called Hilda. Haughey continued, 'The next thing Hilda walked in and wasn't she was a f–king blonde. My own children thought I was a fraud.'

One could not make up the story of the day I had with Charles Haughey at Abbeville. I made a further arrangement with him to return to undertake my research proper.

When I was with Haughey for my second visit, as my interview came to a close, he asked, 'Do you know Basil Blackshaw? I'd like to get him to paint my horse, Flashing Steel.' Flashing Steel had won the Irish Grand National in 1995 and Haughey knew the Northern painter was celebrated for painting horses. I met Basil, whom I knew, to discuss the commission not long after. He grew very excited. He told me, 'You know, Eamonn, I like that aul' horse; I like the flash on his forehead. I watched him in a few races.' He continued, 'You know, around here' – Basil lived up in Antrim – 'they wouldn't be too keen on Haughey, but I'll tell you something, Haughey was the only politician who ever gave me a bit of money. He made me a member of Aosdána [an association of artists whose work is deemed to have made an outstanding contribution to the creative arts in Ireland].' Basil readily agreed to paint Flashing Steel. We arranged to visit Haughey to discuss the details.

On arrival at Abbeville, Haughey met us on the steps in great form, delighted to meet Basil. After a drink in the Malton Room, we sat down to lunch. It wasn't long before the champagne was flowing and the butler was placing silver salvers, covered by silver domes, in front of us. As the lunch progressed, the two men engaged in more serious conversation about their respective horses (Basil usually owned a leg of some horse or other). With more drink consumed, the heads were drawing closer together, bobbing and bobbing, with discussions becoming ever more animated about 'my trainer' and 'your trainer' and so on. It was a rare privilege to sit at that table that day. They could have talked all day, but we still had to go to the Curragh, where Flashing Steel was stabled. Basil was well gone and he still hadn't seen the horse.

Eventually, we headed for the Curragh in the State car. When we arrived, a young stable boy took Basil to see Flashing Steel in his stable, and then backed the horse out into the yard. Throughout the visit, Basil was studying the horse, examining it and checking its conformation. As the stable boy was putting Flashing Steel back into his stall, I spotted Basil ramming his hand deep down into his pocket, pulling out what he used to call a 'rowl' of notes, peeling off a few of them and discreetly feeding them into the stable boy's hand. It was a lovely touch from an absolute gentleman. It was consistent with the generosity and the kindness which I had known in the person of Basil Blackshaw.

By the time we returned to Abbeville to pick up my car, Basil was sobering up. When we were pulling away from the front door of Haughey's residence, I spotted something hanging on the wing mirror of my jeep. When I got out to check what it was, I discovered that it was a large bottle of Veuve Clicquot champagne put there by our host. I joked to Basil, a Protestant, that it was the Holy Viaticum (eucharist in the Catholic Church) for the journey home. We had a wonderful day, and Basil loved it.

Some weeks later, Blackshaw set about painting Flashing Steel. I kept in touch with Haughey and was eventually able to let him know that the work was finished. He arranged with me that I should bring Blackshaw and the painting to Dublin. We arrived at Abbeville and, once in Haughey's foyer, the jollifications kicked off again. 'Let's see the painting,' said Haughey. Basil and I went to the car and brought the work in. Haughey stared at it and stared at it. He turned around to Basil, spat on his hand and asked him to shake. The deal was done the way it used to be done at the horse fairs long ago in Ballinasloe. Charles Haughey was so excited. Of course, we had lunch, and Haughey and Blackshaw had more Veuve Clicquot. Haughey told us that Robert Sangster – the legendary breeder and trainer – had arranged for a case of champagne to be delivered to him that morning.

When it came to payment, Basil asked me how much I thought he should bill Haughey for the painting. I advised him that it was a big commission for a high-profile person, now hanging in an important collection. Basil mentioned a ridiculously low figure to me. I told him I thought he was crazy, and he left it to me to agree a price with Haughey. When I brought Haughey's cheque to Basil, he told me it was 'the biggest lump of money' he'd ever got for a painting. He added, 'I tell you what, I'll do you a wee drawing for you for doing that for me.' Basil accordingly did my portrait. It is not the most flattering, but it is a wonderful piece of art.

Neither Haughey nor Blackshaw is with us any longer. They were two 'rare boys'.

Chapter Ten

The 'Never, Never, Never' Paisley

IN AN INTERVIEW FOR BBC television, the widely respected public servant Dr Maurice Hayes once told me, 'There are six Ian Paisleys. It depends which of them turns up on the day.' I believe that I met all six over the years that I knew Paisley.

My first encounter with Paisley was in 1976, outside his home in Cyprus Avenue, East Belfast. By this time, he was already a major presence on the political landscape. I had been dispatched by my news desk at Downtown Radio to go to his house to get an interview. I met him on the doorstep. When I introduced myself, Paisley asked, 'Where do you come from?'

'South Armagh,' I told him. 'Would you do an interview for me?'

'Why wouldn't I?' he said.

'I thought that because I come from South Armagh, you might not want to talk to me,' I replied. But in fact, from that day until the day he died in September 2014, Ian Paisley and I had a rare rapport, despite our different backgrounds. Like Enoch Powell, Paisley was the quintessential edge-of-society politician and, of course, he fascinated me. He was so enigmatic, such a multi-faceted man. There were few people in public life in Northern Ireland whom I interviewed or recorded more.

Paisley's father, James, had been a member of Edward Carson's UVF and an evangelist. This was the political and religious environment that spawned the young firebrand Paisley. He unapologetically described himself as a 'Reformation Protestant', dedicated to keeping the thoroughfare open for 'our Protestant faith and our Protestant heritage'. Over the years, I listened to Paisley tongue-lashing all his political rivals, nationalists, all shades of unionism, the Catholic Church and the pope. Although he was a committed royalist, he even targeted the Queen Mother and Princess Margaret. He said they had committed 'spiritual fornication and adultery with the Antichrist' because they had had an audience with the pope in 1959. When Pope John XXIII died in 1963, Paisley remarked, 'This Romish man of sin is now in hell!' When Pope John Paul II visited the European parliament in October 1988, Paisley caused uproar in the chamber by shouting across the floor, 'I renounce you, I renounce you as the Antichrist! I refuse you as Christ's enemy and Antichrist with all your false doctrine.'

Nonetheless, of the three major figures in political life in Northern Ireland – John Hume, Gerry Adams and Ian Paisley – Paisley was the most open and affable. There was little small talk from Hume and Adams; they were more the prefects of the class, more cerebral in disposition. Paisley, by contrast, was more vocal, always armed with an arsenal of killer lines. He was not just an orator; he had a knack of burgling the speech-banks of others and turning their words to suit his own purpose. I was outside the DUP headquarters in East Belfast one day and a poor devil, the worse for drink, approached Paisley, slapped him on the back and said, 'Keep it up, big man. Keep it up.' Minutes later, brandishing his fist, Paisley declared to the press conference, 'The man in the street is telling me, "Keep it up, big man. Keep it up, big man."' He had a sharp tongue, but he was wonderfully humorous, and he was a great storyteller in a quintessentially Irish way. On one occasion, when I was walking up Prince of Wales Driveway leading to Parliament Buildings with Paisley, the sole of my shoe had become loose and was making a flapping noise. Paisley stared down at my shoe and said, 'Come on you *spailpín*, you.' *Spailpín* was the Irish word for Traveller; Paisley insisted that it was a great Ballymena word.

He regularly referred to himself as 'my wife's husband'. He was a big child in many ways who liked Kali sucker lollipops and thought nothing of asking a child for a lick of their Mr Whippy ice cream. He was also a man to whom funny things happened. One night, he was returning from London and was met by his bodyguards as he came down the steps of the plane at Belfast International Airport. They picked up his bag as they normally did and whisked him off in his armoured car. As they were approaching Templepatrick roundabout, heading for Belfast, a message came across the radio from another RUC car, asking Paisley's driver to pull in because they had a gentleman in a car behind them who needed to speak urgently with Mr Paisley. Soon, the second RUC car came screeching to a halt behind Paisley's car, followed by another car. The gentleman in the third vehicle had Paisley's bag and Paisley had his. The man, now face to face with Paisley, informed him that he was a salesman for a lingerie firm. 'I don't think it would be very good for you tonight at a meeting in Ballymena to open your bag and find it full of knickers and bras,' he said. I can still hear Paisley roaring with laughter as he told me that story.

While loyal to the Crown, he more often than not detested English politicians, incurring the wrath of British prime ministers over and over again both privately and on the floor in the House of Commons. In fact, I once had a briefing in Margaret Thatcher's private study in Downing Street, the very room in which Paisley told me the Iron Lady had cracked the arm of her chair one night in a bout of bad temper during an exchange with him. Ian Paisley was adjudged for decades to be 'a wrecker', not just at Westminster but also on the island of Ireland and in the European parliament. He was an outlier, a rebel, a dissident ... but ultimately, he changed.

He was, for the greater part of his life, vehemently opposed to the Republic of Ireland. In an outburst against the then taoiseach, Charles J. Haughey, he asked, 'What sort of a self-respecting country would have a prime minister called Hawee, Heehaw?' Much later, in 2003, the DUP leader sparked a major row when he launched a very personal attack on the appearance of Brian Cowen, the Irish minister for foreign affairs. Speaking to DUP colleagues, he said, 'Somebody told me the other day the reason his lips were so thick was that when his mother was bringing him up he was a very disobedient young boy, so she used to put glue on his lips and put him to the floor and keep him there. That has been recorded in his physical make-up.'

From the very get-go, Paisley was endlessly scheming to disrupt and to tear down any political edifice that had any link to Dublin. A British general election was called for 15 October 1964. Republicans nominated Liam McMillan to contest West Belfast for the Irish Republican Party, and a decision was taken to display a tricolour in their Divis Street office window. James Kilfedder, Unionist candidate in West Belfast, complained about the flag – in a telegram to Home Affairs Minister Brian McConnell, he wrote, 'Remove tricolour in Divis Street which is aimed to provoke and insult loyalists of Belfast.' Paisley, who was becoming ever more vociferous against any manifestation of connectedness to Dublin, threatened that if the RUC did not remove the tricolour he would lead a march of his followers to Divis Street and take the flag out of the window. When the police removed the tricolour on Monday 28 September, this provoked rioting by nationalists instead, in response to their action.

Paisley became increasingly vociferous about bolting the door on Dublin and its interest in Northern Ireland at all costs. In 1967, when Terence O'Neill had invited Taoiseach Jack Lynch to Belfast, Paisley and his supporters snowballed their car at Carson's monument at Stormont. After two terms in jail arising from street protesting, his influence in working-class Protestant areas grew, particularly with the emergence of the IRA. He unseated Terence O'Neill, the prime minister, in his North Antrim constituency as MP at Stormont initially, and shortly afterwards snatched his Westminster seat from him. Paisley's son, Ian Junior, holds that seat to this very day. Paisley's next major goal was to bring down the 1973–74 power-sharing executive led by Brian Faulkner, a unionist, with Gerry Fitt of the SDLP as his deputy. This executive had come about as a result of the Sunningdale Agreement, an arrangement which was worked out during negotiations between nationalists and unionists in 1973. The SDLP insisted on a link between the Republic of Ireland and Northern Ireland through what was called the Council of Ireland. The idea of this was anathema to Paisley and loyalist organisations. They turned up the heat with the Ulster Workers' Council Strike of May 1974 and the executive collapsed. At the heart of Paisley's raison d'être was his opposition to any connection with the Republic of Ireland and his contempt for the pope and the Catholic Church. Practically every protest in which he involved himself for the bulk of his political life was driven by these two obsessions.

I was one of a small number of journalists invited by the DUP to the party headquarters on the night of 6 February 1981. From there, we were taken to an unknown destination. At no point were we told where we were going. I had already been party to some hairy republican escapades, travelling to unknown destinations to meet with IRA leaders, but an event of this nature in unionism was a different experience for me. I was completely in the dark. Paisley was protesting against what had been described as 'the totality of relationships' between the two islands following a meeting between Charles Haughey and Margaret Thatcher in December 1980 in Dublin. This new-found harmony had prompted him to act. What followed was broadcast in my report on the early-morning news bulletins – locally, nationally and internationally – the next day, 7 February:

> The night of drama was cloaked in secrecy from the word go. A select number of journalists, David Capper of BBC News NI and Harry Robinson of the *Belfast News Letter* and myself, were asked to come to the DUP headquarters in East Belfast. On our arrival we were informed we would be going on a journey but no indication was given as to where we were going. Having got into two cars, and having been driven for over thirty miles into the County Antrim

countryside, we were still none the wiser about what was to be our experience. When we arrived at a rendezvous point we were directed into a van with blacked-out windows. Half an hour later, we arrived at what seemed to me to be the top of a mountain. Two of the people accompanying us, who kept their faces well concealed, led us across a considerable area of scrubland where, to our surprise, we were met by Ian Paisley dressed in a long, dark tweed coat and wearing a brown hat, something I hadn't seen on him before. To our absolute surprise we could see in the darkness of the night the outline of endless rows of men in army formation. At that point Ian Paisley, like a general, marshalling his troops told us, 'This is only a token of many thousands of men who have pledged to me and I am pledged to them to stand together at this time of grave trouble in Northern Ireland. Every man here is a holder of a legal firearms certificate. Gentlemen, just watch a moment and I will prove that to you,' he said. With my tape recorder still running, Mr Paisley blew a whistle and the men brandished what we were told were legally held gun licences above their heads. We were invited to inspect the five hundred men, who were unmasked, wore no uniforms and behaved in a disciplined fashion. Each one of us, I discovered later, had made a point of counting the rows as we moved along them. With this now over, we were led away back to our waiting van, which had brought us to witness the extraordinary scene in the early hours of the morning.

After we were led away from the hilltop, Paisley read a statement to us to explain further what was going on:

These are men who knowing the greatness of the issues, depending on their faithfulness, have promised each to the other that to the utmost of the strength and means given to them and not regarding any selfish or private interest, their substance, or their lives, they will make a good pledge that they have all entered in to take when called upon, whatever steps are necessary to defeat the present conspiracy to destroy Northern Ireland, hatched at the Government summit.

Paisley denied that any of the men present belonged to the UDA or any other Protestant paramilitary group, but he was not forthcoming about whether any of those present were in the security services. He refused to expand on that. I would have been shocked had there not been someone with links to the security services there. It was an unnerving scene. The experience that night had an echo of history dating back to Carson's UVF era. I felt Paisley, in his every utterance and demeanour, was modelling himself on Carson, his hero.

Paisley's 'Show of Strength' on the Antrim Hills made worldwide headlines. Rhonda – the DUP leader's daughter, who was studying art at the time at the Bob Jones University in Greenville, South Carolina – later told me that there was suddenly a fascination with her because news had reached the US that her father had his 'own army'.

In the wake of the Antrim Hills event, Paisley formed a militia mimicking a people's army, drilling and marching in serried ranks, vowing to defeat the IRA and to block Dublin involvement in the affairs of Northern Ireland. This militia was known as the 'Third Force'. There were huge rallies organised by the DUP leader in practically every major unionist town. I covered almost all of these and was quite often the only Catholic present. One night in north Antrim, when Paisley had the crowd really, really revved up and I was sitting there recording everything, I wondered, will I be savaged here tonight? To my surprise and relief, at just that moment, the DUP leader looked over at me and said, 'Eemonn' – he always pronounced my name that way – 'is a Roman Catholic, but he's all right.' There were scary moments in those days.

What was remarkable was what followed. Between 1981 and 1985, Paisley continued to up the ante in terms of his protests and his anti-British-government rhetoric but – despite all this noise and protest – Thatcher and her Dublin counterpart, Garret FitzGerald, signed the Anglo-Irish Agreement at Hillsborough Castle on 15 November 1985.

Hillsborough Castle was where I had my first exchange with the Iron Lady. I was handed the microphone to put my questions to Thatcher and FitzGerald during the press conference. I put it to Thatcher that Paisley was again threatening that 'Ulster will fight and Ulster will be right'. I asked her, 'Will you stare down Mr Paisley and the loyalists?' Momentarily thinking she was answering an opposition member in the House of Commons, she responded, 'The Honourable Member's question does not surprise me.' It was not one of her finest moments. Secretary of State Tom King was heard to say under his breath, 'To call anybody but Mallie "honourable" ...' He knew Thatcher was hurt, as she would be again in the coming years when I did battle with her.

This growing bond between Dublin and London trauma-tised unionists, who felt Thatcher had betrayed them to such an extent that they burnt effigies of her at rallies. It shocked me to see people who considered themselves part of the Union engaging in this activity – burning one of the most manifest symbols of that Union. One of the biggest unionist crowds ever seen gathered in November 1985 at Belfast City Hall to protest at the signing of the Anglo-Irish Agreement. Paisley boomed to the crowd, 'Where do the terrorists operate from? From the Irish Republic. That's where they come from. Where do the terrorists return to for sanctuary? To the Irish Republic and yet Mrs Thatcher tells us that the Republic must have some say in our Province. We say never, never, never, never.' Later, in December, all fifteen Unionist MPs at Westminster resigned their seats in protest over the agreement, forcing a by-election.

In the summer of 1986, while Paisley was in America on Church business, his deputy, Peter Robinson, participated in another act of protest against the Anglo-Irish Agreement. On 7 August, he led a convoy of supporters on an attempted incursion into the border village of Clontibret, County Monaghan, alleging that security on the border was 'porous' on the southern side. His aim was to demonstrate how easy it was to cross the border unhindered, claiming that there was no will in Dublin to stop the IRA or to improve border security, although it had been promised under the agreement.

The border invaders met in Tandragee, County Armagh, with the aim of travelling together to Clontibret. But many of the boy racers took off at top speed, leaving half the convoy behind, lost in a maze of country roads. Very few of them had ever been in the Republic of Ireland and even fewer were familiar with border country. About 200 of Peter Robinson's 'crack border squad' ended up taking over the tiny hamlet of Glaslough, fifteen miles away from Clontibret. The only sign of life in

Glaslough in the early hours of the morning was a woman who stepped outside her door to see what all the commotion was in the street. She was told by a spokesman for the crowd that they were taking over the village of Clontibret to protest against border security. The woman immediately set the visitors right, telling them they were in the wrong place. Jim Wells, who was there, told me, 'Our map reading was poor!' They had ignored the fundamental rule of scouting – Be Prepared. By then it was too late to head for Clontibret.

On the way home, the DUP members were stopped by the RUC in Armagh. I am told that the boots of some cars contained hoods and baseball bats. The police were told all sorts of tall tales 'about doing a tour of the countryside and so on', and took no action. However, Robinson was arrested by the gardaí and appeared before the Special Criminal Court in Dublin. He was convicted for unlawful assembly and fined IR£17,500. Charges relating to assault on gardaí and malicious damages were dropped.

This became the dominant story of the week. To avoid a prison sentence – and losing his Westminster seat – Robinson pleaded guilty and paid the fine. This gave rise to his being nick-named 'Peter the Punt'. The whole episode ended up as a farce.

Robinson ceased to be deputy leader of the DUP for a short time after this, and Alan Murray of *The Irish Press* got the story. I raced to the Robinson home in Dundonald the morning the story broke to get an interview. It was just after 8 a.m. when I rang the doorbell and one of the Robinson children opened the door. He ran and told his parents that I was there. It has been said that Iris hid under the sheets, believing that I was on my way up the stairs. I had a reputation as a reporter for going where others wouldn't go – but no, I had not considered violating the privacy of the Robinsons' bedroom.

In response to the signing of the Anglo-Irish Agreement, another unionist force was mobilised; it was called the Ulster Resistance Movement and its members wore red berets. Robinson – now reinstated as Paisley's deputy – was the prime mover behind this organisation. The beret-wearing was a gift for satirists like Danny Morrison, who wickedly said of Ian Paisley, 'He was the fool on the hill in the middle of the night waving firearms certificates at the moon. He was a swaggering Idi Amin in his red beret as he marched Ulster Resistance, yet another of his Third Forces, round in circles. He was the boyo who was going to smash Sinn Féin!'

From a unionist perspective, the period from 1986 to 1993 was a barren one in politics in Northern Ireland, with little compromise or give by the British government about the Anglo-Irish Agreement. Unionist politicians grew increasingly sullen and sour in the face of what they perceived as intransigence in Downing Street.

Taoiseach Albert Reynolds, who with John Major was one of the authors of the Downing Street Declaration in 1993, enquired of Father Brian D'Arcy if he knew anybody who could set up a meeting between him and Ian Paisley on a possible political way ahead. Father D'Arcy, who was very active all his life in the music industry, suggested Reynolds should put a call through to his old Ballymena friend, dance-hall owner Sammy Barr, who knew Paisley well. According to Reynolds, Barr was blunt and to the point: 'Paisley will only do a deal when he is number one.' How prophetic this was. Having walked the highways and byways of Northern Ireland with the DUP leader for most of my professional life, I did not ever detect the slightest clue that he would contemplate forming a government or being in a government with republicans, having pledged over and over again to 'smash Sinn Féin'.

The Downing Street Declaration, which addressed some of the issues such as the right of the people on the island of Ireland to self-determination, was a significant step in nudging republicanism further down the road to constitutional politics and acted ultimately as a stepping-stone to the ceasefires in 1994 and to the Good Friday Agreement. That IRA ceasefire, followed by the loyalist ceasefire, changed everything – and sooner or later Paisley would have to come to terms with a new situation in Northern Ireland where Sinn Féin was emerging as a serious political force, espousing constitutional politics.

Nothing I was hearing from Ian Paisley during the 1990s indicated that he was mellowing in any way. The DUP and unionism had effectively been at loggerheads with Downing Street since the Anglo-Irish Agreement in 1985. Bellicose outbursts made by Paisley at Castle Buildings on the Stormont Estate during the making of the Good Friday Agreement did not augur well for the taming of the DUP leader. Those 1998 negotiations were seen as just the newest political pill administered by the British and Irish governments for the DUP to swallow. Paisley unambiguously told me that year, 'I am totally opposed to gunmen who have not given up their weaponry and to be able to sit at the Cabinet table and to rule the country. It is madness.'

Despite their opposition to the Good Friday Agreement, which was embraced by a majority in Northern Ireland, the Assembly election of 2003 saw the DUP emerge as the biggest party in Northern Ireland with thirty seats. The following year, Paisley's party was the biggest Northern Irish party at Westminster, now that Jeffrey Donaldson had abandoned the UUP to join them. With the growth in the vote of the DUP and of Sinn Féin from 2003 onwards, the British and Irish governments knew with certainty that the so-called 'parties of the extremes' needed to be brought into the fold.

Three weeks before the interparty conference at St Andrews in Scotland in October 2006 came a seminal moment. I was having breakfast with Paisley at his home when he said, 'Eemonn, before I expire I want to see everybody in Northern Ireland working together.' I was stunned. It was the first time I heard him indicating that he might be up for a deal. 'Does this include Sinn Féin?' I asked. 'Yes, they have the vote and they are not going away. That is democracy,' he said.

The St Andrews talks of 11–13 October were not easy. There were those in the DUP who were now concluding that Ian Paisley was moving too quickly and was too willing to make concessions to republicanism. Among those who were seeking to pull the handbrake on Paisley was Nigel Dodds, who was reportedly arguing for a longer period before going into government with Sinn Féin to test the bona fides of republicans on all fronts. However, Paisley – who was accompanied by his wife, Eileen, and his son, Ian Junior, at the St Andrews talks – was in a buoyant mood throughout.

That particular weekend was the Paisleys' fiftieth wedding anniversary, and the family was hosting a special evening at Barnett Demesne in South Belfast, where the couple had held their wedding reception. To mark the occasion, the Irish government had shrewdly brought a gift for the Paisleys that became known as 'the Bertie bowl'. It had a major resonance for Ian Paisley as it had been carved from a fallen oak tree from the banks of the River Boyne where King Billy won his famous battle over King James. I can still see Paisley's face wreathed in smiles, admiring the bowl in the chamber at St Andrews, both delighted with the gift and, I suspected, tickled by the irony of it. He was like a child with a new toy at Christmas. To this day, the Paisleys will brook no criticism of Bertie Ahern.

As the talks at St Andrews ran on that Friday, the Paisleys were becoming increasingly worried that they might not make it home in time for their anniversary party. Tony Blair quickly solved that problem. Having suggested to Paisley that his presence was critical for several hours more, he suggested to him that he and Mrs Paisley could share the secretary of state's plane back to Belfast that evening. The Paisleys had reason to be happy – flying home in luxury in time for their party. By now, all the pieces of the jigsaw were starting to fall into place. The IRA had put their weapons beyond use and republicans were supporting the PSNI (the proposed new Police Service of Northern Ireland) and had pledged their support for the judicial system in Northern Ireland. Paisley, at the end of the St Andrews conference, made a very optimistic statement when he said, 'I trust that we will see in the coming days the vast majority of people taking the road of democracy.'

There was only one turn of the wheel left, and that was for Paisley to go into government with republicans. Come May 2007, he became first minister, with Martin McGuinness as his deputy, in a new Assembly and executive at Parliament Buildings. The remarkable friendship that developed between the DUP leader and the former IRA leader symbolised the hope of a new beginning in the eyes of many. Paisley and McGuinness were regularly caught on camera guffawing and chuckling. Before long, they were given the nickname 'The Chuckle Brothers'. There has been much speculation about who came up with it. According to David McNarry, the former Ulster Unionist member of the Northern Ireland Assembly, it was Andy Tyrie Junior, son of loyalist Andy Tyrie, who coined the phrase when he said to McNarry one night at an Orange Lodge meeting, 'What about the Chuckle Brothers?' The next day, McNarry sidled up to the BBC's political correspondent Martina Purdy in the Great Hall in Parliament Buildings and said to her, 'Do you know what they are calling the two boys Paisley and McGuinness up here now?' UUP assembly member Danny Kennedy dropped the sobriquet into an interview he was doing, and it very quickly became currency. Little did we know at the time that the Paisley–McGuinness 'marriage' would result in an earthquake not just within the party which Ian Paisley founded, but also in the Free Presbyterian Church that he established.

Chapter Eleven

Paisley and I

PAISLEY'S DECISION TO GO into government with Sinn Féin fascinated everyone, and especially me. Why this road-to-Damascus conversion? Why had Paisley now felt ready to acknowledge the legitimacy of republicans in government – working closely with Martin McGuinness, for example – against the backdrop of his lifelong antipathy and disdain for them? I had so many in-depth questions to put to Paisley about his actions over the decades, and for this reason I had been asking him over and over again if he would work with me to write his biography.

Every time I raised the topic of a book with Paisley, he would reply, 'A man from Crossmaglen writing my biography? Do you want to get me shot, Eemonn?' I didn't give up, though. In spring 2012, Ian Paisley Junior dropped in at our home in South Belfast, as he did from time to time. I casually asked him whether there was any sign of his father recording his life story or doing any writing about his life, now that he had left the public stage. Junior told me that, as a family, they were so disappointed because they could not get his father to focus on such a project.

The next morning, my phone rang. It was Rhonda, Ian's

sister. She told me that her mum and dad would like me to come to see them. I was immediately excited, especially given the conversation I'd had with Ian Junior. I didn't hang around – I was on the Paisleys' doorstep within an hour. Once I was inside, without much preamble, Paisley said he was ready to write his life story and asked me if I would help. I didn't answer straight away. I'd been thinking a lot about the project since that phone call. I was very conscious that Paisley was well into his eighties and – whilst he had written a lot of pamphlets and short books over the years – I wondered if he realised just how much work would be involved in a biography. I had started to think that the better approach would be to do my research and then interview him on camera about all the different periods of his life. I asked him for a few moments to reflect. I joined Mrs Paisley and Rhonda in the kitchen and ran my suggestion past them – a television programme rather than a book. They both immediately saw the merit in this approach. We then joined Paisley in his snug. I put my proposal to him, and both his wife and daughter rowed in behind me. He didn't hesitate in accepting the idea.

This was my first major venture after I had stopped working as a frontline reporter, and I was determined that it would be an independent production. To sit down and interrogate one of the most controversial figures ever in Northern Ireland politics would be one of the biggest coups of my career. I asked the Paisleys to put in writing that they were granting me the rights to their life story, which they did straight away. I then went directly to the controller of the BBC, Peter Johnston. When I told him about the planned interview, he replied, 'If you can get Ian Paisley to tell his unvarnished life story, we have no choice but to work with you because we need him for the archives. We approached him through a number of channels, inviting him to share his life story with us, but to no avail.' I assured Peter I could deliver. By this time, our son, Michael, was home from England for a break. Aware of the scale of the project, I was in no doubt that I would need a lot of help, and where better to ask than at home? I invited Michael to come on-board and he agreed.

I spent the next months researching and interviewing Mrs Paisley and members of the immediate family. I wanted to know everything about Paisley – every manifestation of his life. Both his son Kyle and daughter Rhonda were critical reference points throughout this period. Once I felt I'd done most of my research, I decided to deliver a presentation to make sure I had covered all the bases. Ian and Eileen Paisley, Rhonda, Michael and I convened at Bannside Library, which is dedicated to Paisley and houses about 5,000 of his books. I spoke for close to one hour – I wanted to run past them everything that I considered relevant and make sure I hadn't missed anything. When I'd finished, I asked Paisley if he had any comments. 'Don't forget that silly ass Robinson and Clontibret,' was the only remark he made. It was after that meeting that we set a date for filming for autumn 2012.

As we edged towards that date, we visited the Paisleys to address some housekeeping matters vis à vis what the DUP leader would wear during each interview, the duration of the interviews and so on. Michael and I had just sat down with the Paisleys for our discussion when, to everybody's surprise as far as I could gauge, we were joined by another member of the family. That individual started to interrogate us about conditions, terms, etc., around the interviews. Eileen Paisley cut short this intervention, outlining the confidence she and her husband had in Michael and me. That said, the input of that family member was something of a shock and put us in an invidious position where we felt we had to justify ourselves in some way. As we left the Paisley house we were quite shaken in the wake of what just taken place. It meant the commencement of the interviews the following Tuesday had to go on hold.

On our way home I started to feel distinctly unwell. Michael noticed and asked me if I was all right. In fact, I felt as if I was outside myself, and my short-term memory was a bit hazy. As soon as I got home, Detta gave me something to eat as I'd had nothing since lunchtime. As I tried to eat, I knew something was seriously wrong – I felt I didn't have any short-term recall. Michael rushed me straight to the doctors' surgery. It was closed, so we went directly to A & E at the Royal Victoria Hospital. I was kept in overnight. In the early hours of the morning, and after several blood tests, a young doctor told me that I had suffered an 'acute cardiac event'. I asked whether this meant I'd had a bad heart attack. 'Yes,' she replied.

At 8.30 a.m., my son-in-law, Gerard Rafferty, a consultant who studied cardiology for a time before switching to gastroenterology, called me and asked me to take him through my symptoms. To my great relief, he said he didn't believe it had been a heart attack. At 2 p.m., the consultant, Mr Dalzell, arrived to tell me that I hadn't suffered a heart attack but that I would have to have a series of tests due to my memory lapse. As I lay in my bed, feeling pretty down and disappointed at this turn of events, I decided I would close the screens around the bed to try to shut out the world. This was easier said than done – there was a man in the bed opposite me whom I found very irritating. I was quite upset at the tone he used when he was speaking to his wife on the phone, and at his use of bad language. Some time later, I spotted a priest visiting him. I was worried that the priest might next approach my bed. I was very preoccupied with the clerical child-abuse scandal at that time. I knew I would have to express my opinion on this matter should the priest join me. I watched the clergyman coming to the middle of the floor. I assumed he would head next to my bed, but he suddenly pivoted, swung right and left me in peace.

Minutes later, Rhonda Paisley rang. I told her I was in hospital and she asked me to hold on, and Paisley came on the phone asking what had happened. Once I told him, he said, 'Let's say a prayer,' and was soon invoking God's blessing and asking for a speedy recovery for me. I thanked him and I told him I would be in touch. You could not have made this up. A priest from the Catholic faith in which I was brought up was within feet of my bed and walked off, and the next thing the former moderator of the Free Presbyterian Church was on the phone praying for me.

Around this time, I began to get calls from colleagues, asking what had happened. It transpired that a well-known Sinn Féin member from North Belfast was in a side ward in the hospital. As I was being wheeled up the corridor, he spotted me and called Danny Morrison, who started ringing around my colleagues, asking if I was all right. Very quickly, the word had spread. It was a bad day for those with shares in Mallie Inc., but I made a full recovery, thanks be to God. I put what had happened to me down to stress.

I took a short break, and then we set a new start date for the filming. Our friends at PI Communications, Norah-Anne and Conor O'Brien, provided us with recording gear, cameras and manpower; the former head of news and current affairs at BBC Northern Ireland, Andrew Colman, came on board as executive producer. In the lead-in to recording the Paisleys, Detta and the family and I had taken a few days out in Kelly's Hotel in Rosslare, County Wexford. Detta and I walked for hours along the wonderful shoreline there. I took her through Paisley's life, chapter and verse, to reinforce my recollection of the facts. I was testing my recall all the time. I also watched the famous Frost/ Nixon interviews over and over again to study David Frost's modus operandi. It was a profitable exercise. Frost had his own money riding on the Nixon interviews. Having recorded hours and hours of the former president, he hadn't gleaned a single news line of any consequence from Richard Nixon about the whole Watergate scandal. I was determined not to find myself in the same situation. Although it had been a coup to get the interview, I now needed to maximise all its potential.

Our recordings of Ian Paisley were to be done sub rosa, absolutely secretly. No one, except for our very small team, had any idea about what was happening. We went to extreme lengths to keep it like that so that when the news of the interviews broke, the impact would be so much the greater.

The filming would continue for close to six months, with each session lasting about an hour. We were mindful that Paisley was no longer a young man. There was a ritual each time we arrived at the Paisleys' home. While the crew set up, Rhonda had the kettle on the boil and Paisley got into the same suit and tie that he would wear throughout, for continuity. We were filming in the library at the Paisleys' home, probably one of the finest private libraries on this island. I hadn't ever seen so many Bibles in my life – there were dozens of them. Paisley was so proud of his full collection of blue-bound Ussher volumes: rare books of writings and sermons by James Ussher, the Church of Ireland Archbishop of Armagh and Primate of All Ireland between 1625 and 1656. Eileen Paisley told me that she had bought the collection as a Christmas present for her husband.

Paisley bought books all over the world. Wherever he went, he would ask his drivers to take him to bookshops, where he would hoke through the stock in pursuit of religious texts by some of his favourite preachers. He bought books that were hundreds of years old. He took them home, dusted them and put them into a sealed container with baking soda. He claimed that this got rid of any musty smell. During the interview, it was not unusual for Paisley to pick up a Bible and start reading from it. Practically every line in any Bible that I examined in the Paisley library was underscored in pencil. He had a photographic memory and appeared to be able to recall what was written on every page without opening the book.

We were keen to convey the atmosphere of that remarkable library – with such an array of books, furniture and rugs – and the acoustics in the room were perfect. Throughout the weeks of interviewing, my son Michael, in his role as producer/director, sat on my right; cameraman Willie John Crawford had his camera fixed on me, at a 45-degree angle, and he also took care of a second camera; senior cameraman Sam Wilson focused his lens on Paisley. Eileen sat to my left, slightly behind me, with an iPad and Apple pencil, taking notes. Michael instructed me that under no circumstances was I to worry about anything else that was happening in the library – my only duty was to look at Paisley, listen to what he was saying and ask the questions. This was exactly what I did during each recording. The routine was like clockwork ... until one day, close to the end of the recordings, I saw out of the corner of my eye that Michael was becoming very preoccupied by something that was happening behind me. Suddenly he shouted, 'Stop, Dad, stop!' I turned immediately to check what was going on. Sam Wilson was stretched out motionless across a chair. At that moment, I thought he was dead. Michael and I carried him into the kitchen and laid him out flat on the floor. Rhonda immediately called the emergency services, while Eileen rushed to get a glass of water. Paisley joined us in the kitchen, white as a ghost, and sat down by the door. I was in a panic. I couldn't detect any signs of life. At that point I asked Paisley to say a prayer or put his hands on Sam. Just then, to our enormous relief, our cameraman came round and – ever the professional – muttered, 'Push that button. Push that button.'

We got some water into him and he sat up. Michael instructed me to disappear, knowing that the ambulance was coming. We had been secretly filming these interviews and we didn't want anybody to see me in the Paisley home in case they put two and two together. What must the dispatcher who took the call from Rhonda Paisley have thought when she reported this emergency involving 'Sam Wilson' in the Paisley household? Thankfully Sam made a good recovery and was back to work in no time.

❋ ❋ ❋

From the outset, I had decided that I wanted to take Paisley through his life chapter by chapter, and one of the early topics about which I was particularly keen to question him was the civil rights movement. When I began to press Paisley about the discrimination against Catholics that had led to the civil rights movement in the late 1960s, he stonewalled me, refusing to concede that discrimination had occurred.

I continued to push him, quoting statistics. I pointed out that out of 330 social houses in Dungannon that had become available, not one had been given to a Catholic. I reminded him that in a city like Derry, where there was a majority of nationalists, the unionists had held sixty-two seats and the nationalists just thirty-two due to gerrymandering. I hammered him for more than an hour on these issues but got nowhere. As Paisley retreated into his snug after that session, I said to Michael that we would have to talk to him – I felt that the last hour had been a waste of time and that I was getting very little back.

When we went into the snug, Eileen Paisley and Rhonda were there too. I told them I felt as though Paisley had been building moats and fortresses around himself during the interview, refusing to address what history had recorded. After a pause, he replied, 'All right – we'll do it tomorrow.' I felt it had been a bad day – this was the first big subject we'd tackled, and the way he'd responded didn't augur well for the many other subjects I wanted to address. When we returned the next day, Paisley was frosty. He didn't say, 'Good morning, men. How are you today?' as he normally did. He sat down in the chair without speaking. I returned to the civil rights era and revisited the allegations of discrimination against Catholics. He remained cold and still wasn't giving much away. To my complete amazement, Eileen Paisley intervened. She said to her husband, 'Look, dear, just admit it, there was wholesale discrimination against Catholics. It's a fact.' Paisley seemed even more taken aback by this intervention than I was. When I repeated my questions, however, he replied, 'The whole system was wrong. It wasn't one man, one vote. It wasn't fair. Fair government is that every man has the same power to vote for what he wants.' He continued, 'It wasn't acceptable at all, it wasn't justice at all. Those who put their hands to that have to carry some of the brunt and blame for what happened in our country. If you vote down democracy, you are responsible for bringing in anarchy and they brought in anarchy and they set family against family and friend against friend.'

I was shocked by his apparent change of heart after all these years. I then asked, 'Why then, did you oppose the civil rights movement? Wasn't that exactly what they were seeking, the right to houses and the right for one man, one vote?' Paisley pushed back, saying, 'Because the civil rights movement was a movement that was actually a United Ireland movement. They were associating with a battle that ordinary, decent Protestants could not be identified with.'

I challenged him: 'How can you say that about people like Austin Currie and John Hume – that they were United Irelanders, given that what they were seeking were British rights, the right to one man one vote, and a decent home?' Paisley stuck to his contention that the civil rights campaign at the time was a front for a United Ireland movement. He also drew attention to deficits in rights for homeless, working-class Protestants – a situation that, disgracefully, hasn't changed much in the intervening years.

By any standards, I figured the former DUP leader had gone further in admitting to the abuses visited by the unionist State upon nationalists than any other unionist politician over the years. Little did I know, though, that this was only a foretaste of the most extraordinary revelations that would emerge over the coming weeks and months.

Another interesting fact emerged when we discussed the aftermath of the 2003 elections. I asked Eileen, 'Were you in any sense trying to persuade your husband to reach an accommodation with republicans to avoid ongoing turmoil in Northern Ireland?' She replied, 'Yes, we discussed it, we discussed it, we prayed about it. We talked round it and through it and in and out and how we could lose friends, and probably would, but we thought the country has come through such a terrible time and people from right across the board had been hurt and damaged beyond all description, and we felt we can't continue that. And also we felt unless an accommodation had been reached it would have been another thirty or forty years and maybe it would have been worse, the whole country would have been on fire.'

This was the first time I learned that such conversations had been taking place within the four walls of the Paisleys' home. So it was against this fresh thinking that the all-party talks at Leeds Castle in September 2004 had taken place. This had been the first important opportunity for Tony Blair to seriously engage with Ian Paisley. During my interview, I learned that the two men had spent some considerable time discussing religion. Paisley said, 'Through matters that were brought up and matters about his grandfather being an Orangeman and that his grandmother was a very, very strong supporter of mine, I learned she once said to Blair, "You don't do anything on Ian Paisley because it would be very unlucky for you if you do."'

After the Leeds Castle meeting, Paisley had issued an upbeat statement in which he said, 'Decommissioning of all IRA weapons and dismantling of the structures of terrorism is the ultimate outcome of this process.' Both the British and Irish governments had left Leeds Castle in a rather optimistic mood, but there was consternation in Dublin and London in October 2004 when Paisley made a statement in which he demanded that the IRA wear 'sackcloth and ashes' by way of repentance. I asked him why he had used that phrase. 'They had to repent and they had to ask forgiveness of the people for the awful state that they had brought Northern Ireland into. It is quite in keeping with what a gospel preacher would say that if you are going to repent you need to do it in sackcloth and ashes. It is a scriptural statement,' he said. In spite of this answer, it was quite conceivable to me that in using this phrase Paisley was targeting a particular audience, mindful of certain elements within his own ranks. Presuming Paisley genuinely believed in the Bible from which he quoted so frequently, seeing it both as a weapon to defend himself or to use to attack others, I can only say I envied him the comfort of having such deep faith.

At no point did we ever give Paisley a list of questions, but I did give advance notice of the topics we would cover in the following week. I guarded that integrity of the line of questioning the whole way through – and, in fairness to the Paisleys, they didn't ever try to find out more about the questions in advance. Inevitably, we were coming to the moment when I would finally be able to ask Paisley about going into government with Sinn Féin. It was when I asked him about this that, to my surprise, he lifted a prepared statement and read:

Over and over again, coming up in this interview and in other interviews we have the word 'the deal' used, and I think that having listened to the various definitions made of the deal by others, it is time that I had the opportunity just to say exactly what this deal was about. They did deal with their weapons and they did accept the principle of consent. I needed republicans to accept the PSNI and the rule of law in Northern Ireland. I was told this never could happen and my response was unless it did, we would never be able to move forward. It did happen. I had to put my best foot forward. I had to put a smile on my face and do what I was elected to do: give leadership.

The fact that he had so carefully nailed down his thinking in this prepared statement showed that he didn't want to risk any ambiguity or misinterpretation of his position. He was determined to let his critics know that he hadn't surrendered to the IRA.

When I asked him if he did the deal in the interest of his legacy, as alleged by many people, Paisley answered, 'No, not at all. My work was as a Christian minister and that always came first. I had to take a step, a step that I had a lot of heart searching on, a step that brought me a lot of pain, a step that had to put me out of the class of a coward into the class of a man that was prepared to sell himself and his reputation for the sake of his country.'

When I pressed him on what he meant when he said that he had to sell himself, he replied, 'I had to sell myself to a lot of criticism of people who didn't know what was really happening and I mean I was blamed for being a Lundy and all sorts of things, but when I look back, you know, he that laughs last, laughs the longest.'

***

What came across at different times during the interviews was Paisley's sense of mischief and the pleasure he derived from winding up his political enemies. One of the most amusing anecdotes he shared with me involved Prime Minister Harold Wilson. At the height of the Ulster Workers' Council Strike. Wilson flew into Northern Ireland for a private meeting with the leader of the DUP, his colleague Billy Beattie and legal advisor Desmond Boal. The talks took place in an upstairs room in Parliament Buildings, looking out over Belfast and Black Mountain. Paisley spoke of a glorious, sunny afternoon, with strong rays of the sun streaming into the room in which the Wilson encounter was taking place. He described to me with great glee the extremes to which they went to discombobulate the prime minister. Harold Wilson had very short legs, according to Paisley, so they invited him to sit on a high, shiny, leather-backed armchair, his legs dangling in mid-air, positioned so that the sun would hit him right in the eyes. Paisley told me that as he and his colleagues berated and pounded Wilson, he took out his pipe and attempted to light it several times as he kept sliding down the chair. Exasperated at the abuse coming at him from all sides, the prime minister eventually put his pipe back in his pocket. Paisley, laughing heartily, described 'a chimney of smoke billowing from Wilson's coat pocket' shortly afterwards. I couldn't stand this story up with Eileen or anyone else, so it wasn't included in the documentaries we made.

However, it was too good a story to forget so I decided to try to find Desmond Boal to see if he could verify it. I tracked him down to a coffee shop in Holywood, County Down, but unfortunately it was packed. The only available seat was at the furthest point away from where Boal was sitting. I decided – Commissaire Maigret-style – to work my way discreetly down the floor as seats became available. The process was slow but successful. Eventually, when two ladies entered the coffee shop, Boal and his friend stood up in readiness for the off. I made my move and spoke to him. 'Now, Eamonn, you know I don't talk to the press,' he said. 'I only ever talked to you at Leopardstown Races.' I reminded him that I had been a member of the press then too. 'Yes,' he said, 'I always saw you [as] a cut above the rest.' I then asked my question about the Harold Wilson story. Wreathed in smiles, he confirmed Paisley's account.

Although Boal clearly enjoyed recalling that meeting with Harold Wilson, by the time I tracked him down in Holywood, he and Paisley had been estranged for some years. In fact, the first significant friendship that Paisley lost after going into government with Martin McGuinness was Desmond Boal's. Boal was a founding member of the DUP and a close confidant of Paisley for practically all his political life. The Paisley children even had a nickname for him. Once when he arrived, Ian and Eileen Paisley were eating their evening meal with their young daughters, Rhonda and Sharon. Boal joked to Eileen, 'I didn't know you allowed pigs at the table.' From that day onwards, the children nicknamed him 'Pig Boal'.

Eileen Paisley painted a graphic picture of the moment that Desmond Boal arrived at the Paisleys' home to terminate their friendship. She told me, 'He came up the driveway with the books that Ian had given him. He said, "This isn't a friendly visit. I just can't believe he has done what he has done. I don't want anything more to do with you.'" She replied, "'Well, Desmond, I am very sorry it has come to that. Ian had to do what he had to do. What could he do? Would you have him be responsible for another thirty or forty years of warfare and devastation and killing and murdering or do what he did?" I don't think he answered. He just walked away. It was a very big blow to Ian, a very big blow, and we do miss him. He was a great character and he was great fun and he was a lovely person to come in and have as a friend and we had a very close relationship.' That breach was not healed before Ian Paisley's death in September 2014.

Boal's reaction to Paisley being in government with Martin McGuinness would presage turbulence in both the Free Presbyterian Church and in the DUP. As soon as Ian Paisley had agreed to go into government with Martin McGuinness as his deputy, red lights started flashing in the church of which Paisley was moderator. Free Presbyterian minister and former close colleague Ivan Foster led a delegation from the Free Presbyterian Church to Parliament Buildings to protest in person against Paisley's dual role as moderator and first minister. This dual role became the subject of heated debate at presbytery meetings within the Church in the spring of 2007.

Having spent so much time researching the life of the Paisleys, it had quickly become clear to me that two issues were going to dominate our interviews – the Church which he founded dumping him, and the party which he had also founded killing him off as party leader and sequentially First Minister. I began by asking Paisley, 'Did you think that what was emerging had the potential to split the Church?' He replied, 'I regret that they have not the ear of God on this matter. I don't see them crowding into their prayer meetings. I don't see them taking the matter in prayer, but they can pour all their fury on me and I am broad enough in the shoulders and my stomach is strong enough to take all of the condemnations they want.'

The campaign inside the Free Presbyterian Church came to a head in September 2007 at the Church's annual general meeting of the presbytery in Martyrs' Memorial in East Belfast. It was at that meeting each year that the moderator was elected. For fifty years, Paisley's leadership had gone unchallenged. Even though he had met with some hostility at a number of presbytery meetings, his family did not initially believe that his moderatorship would be under any serious threat. Moves were afoot, however, to put pressure on Paisley to step back from his role as moderator of the Church, the argument being that double-jobbing as first minister and moderator was incompatible.

The uproar at the meeting that night would effectively split the Church but had the BBC's political correspondent Martina Purdy not been covering it, news might not have broken so quickly about the trouble brewing. Eileen Paisley said, 'There was no reason why he should stand down as moderator. He was doing a good job and had done so all his life and there was nothing to stop him continuing with that and continuing with his position as first minister, but the poison had been laid and sprayed and I think that was the damage that had been done.' The vehemence of her language shocked me to the core, mindful of the fact that she was speaking about key figures in the Church, who had been side by side with her husband as moderator for decades.

Kyle Paisley, who is himself a rather docile individual, and a Free Presbyterian minister, told me during my research about the atmosphere in the family home the night before that famous presbytery meeting: 'Dad said, "I never thought in all my life I would be attending a meeting of this kind".'

Eileen Paisley continued to be devastating in the interview in her tirade against her husband's former colleagues in the Church: 'We were not defeated by our enemies but betrayed by our friends.' The mild-mannered Kyle went even further when he summed up his feelings in these words: 'The family just felt as if we had all been stabbed. They seemed to have done it with such consummate ease. We were definitely let down and betrayed.'

The assault on the Church during my interviews was relentless. Paisley himself said, 'I mean there are people and all they wanted was the defeat of the IRA, that was it, and the Protestants who were killing and bombing as well, they are forgotten about. I mean let's be absolutely honest, what should happen is that every person should be subjected to the law.' His wife concluded by saying, 'Our hearts were all broken for Ian, the children and myself as well, and I felt he had been deeply wounded in the house of his friends and I just felt that it was really iniquitous of them and a really dreadful, hurtful, nasty, ungodly, unchristian thing to do.'

What fascinated me throughout the interviews was the fact that historically the Paisleys had reserved this kind of incendiary language for their enemies: republicans, the Vatican and the Irish government. All the time, I wondered would there come a day when the Paisleys regretted the vitriol they were directing at their erstwhile friends?

There would be one more twist to come within Ian Paisley's

Martyrs' Memorial church. In the second half of 2011, Paisley received a letter signed by all members of his church's kirk session demanding that he relinquish his role as minister and cease preaching in the pulpit from which he had delivered sermons for over fifty years. Eileen Paisley said of that letter: 'We were absolutely shattered. We just could not believe that Ian, after sixty-five years ministering in the same church, continuous ministering for all these years, in leading the church and building it, that these men take this attitude and all of a sudden want to boot him out. We just could not fathom it. We just couldn't understand why. In fact one of them said he was destroying the church. He was wrecking the church, that was his term.'

Paisley himself said, 'It was hurtful and that was the way they thought they would treat us and they did that. They will have to answer to the people and they will also have to answer to God at the end of the day.' Paisley announced his retirement in early autumn. He delivered his final address in the pulpit in the Martyrs' Memorial church on the last Sunday in December 2011. The presbytery announced that a meeting would take place in January to mark Paisley's role as former moderator of the Free Presbyterian Church and as minister in Martyrs' Memorial. The church was jam-packed. It was the end of an era for Paisley in the church he had founded. In reality, however, his troubles were only starting.

In February 2012, Paisley became seriously ill and was admitted to the intensive-care unit at the Ulster Hospital. It reached the point where discussions about his funeral were under way. Eileen Paisley told me, 'For four days he was just hovering between life and death in intensive care. He was allowed out of intensive care on the ninth day, but those were four very heavy and oppressing days for us.' What became evident in the interviews for the documentaries was the fact that she laid the blame for this serious illness squarely at the door of the Free Presbyterian Church. Against the odds, Paisley pulled through, forcing his obituarists to rewrite their scripts. Commenting on her husband's departure from his former church, Mrs Paisley said, 'I know Ian was heartbroken and I believe that it was heartbreak that made him ill, took a toll on his health.'

***

On the back of the uprising inside the Free Presbyterian Church in September 2007, I was interested to establish from Eileen Paisley whether they feared that there might be a parallel insurrection inside the DUP. She told me, 'I detected a nasty spirit arising from some of the other MPs and in the way they spoke to Ian. I was very annoyed one day with the way some of those spoke to him and addressed him. Whenever they said something to him about what was going on and he said, "Well, that's what should be done," they said, "Ach Doc, you know, just sort of, don't be so stupid, you know." That sort of set the alarm bells ringing in my head and there was an undergoing current that balls were being made and some of these men were doing the firing of them.'

By now I was becoming accustomed to revelation after revelation in each recording, and there was more to come. According to Paisley, in the wake of the upheaval in the Free Presbyterian Church in 2007, he asked the general secretary of the DUP, Timmy Johnston, to take an informal sounding of the mood within the party. Some time later, Paisley was handed a document by Johnston – it was an audit of his leadership, posing seven questions for DUP Assembly members. The document detailed responses. Five of the questions within this so-called attitude survey addressed Paisley's leadership. Question 3 of the survey read as follows: 'How well do you think Dr Paisley has been performing over the last year?' Question 4 read, 'What are the issues that concern you about Dr Paisley's performance?' Eighty-three per cent of those surveyed felt Paisley should go. The document was signed by Timothy Johnston. In the interview, Paisley was adamant that he had not asked for this.

I could only imagine the scene in the family home that night when Paisley got home and produced this document. Eileen Paisley told me, 'I was furious. To put it mildly, I felt like taking it and ramming it down Timothy Johnston's throat.' When I asked Paisley what the survey was all about, he said, 'Getting rid of Ian Paisley ... in the interest of the people who took over.' Reacting to the outcome of the survey and what was in it, and the questions and answers, Paisley said, 'They were disgraceful, they were absolutely disgraceful. They were disgraceful because the man that they put in my position couldn't keep his own seat in Westminster.' This was an excoriating reference to his former chief lieutenant, Peter Robinson, who became leader and lost his East Belfast Westminster seat in 2010 to the Alliance Party's Naomi Long. 'My son, who followed me, had a marvellous victory [in North Antrim] and for once we are seeing the true nature of the beast, that there was a beast here who was prepared to go forward to the destruction of the party because losing seats in Northern Ireland is a very serious thing. And for

East Belfast not to be a unionist seat in the House of Commons is a terrible, terrible blow.'

Just one week after Paisley had received the survey, a fatal meeting was held during which his future was sealed. That meeting took place in Stormont Castle. Those present included Nigel Dodds, Peter Robinson, Maurice Morrow (party chairman) and Timothy Johnston. According to Paisley, 'Nigel said to me, "We want you to be gone by Friday." I just more or less smirked. Peter said, "Oh no, no, no ... you need to stay in for another couple of months."'

Eileen Paisley did not pull her punches about how Ian's colleagues treated her husband at that meeting. She said, 'He came in and he leaned over the chair and he said, "The mighty Dodds wants me to go by the end of the week." I said, "He's a cheeky sod to ask you to do any such thing," and I said, "What authority has he?" and I was angry and shocked because I thought of how he had been treated by Ian in Europe. He had given him his post [as Paisley's chief advisor] to encourage him and then this is the thanks he gets at the end of the day.'

I then asked her, 'How would you characterise what the leadership did to your husband?'

'I think they assassinated him by their words and by their deeds and by the way they treated him. I think they treated him shamefully,' she replied.

Eileen Paisley had scarcely uttered these words when I envisaged them jumping out from the front page of the *Belfast Telegraph* well ahead of the release of the documentary. The DUP leader and first minister stood down on 4 March 2008.

***

My integrity as a journalist had to be protected at all times – as had the integrity of the commissioning organisation, the BBC. For that reason, I was duty bound to inform the DUP of what was going to be said about the party in the documentary. When I showed the survey document addressing Ian Paisley's competence to Timothy Johnston, the party's general secretary, in the run-up to the broadcast, I pointed out to him that his name was on it. He did not push back on this, stating, 'If my name is on the document then I am responsible for the document.' I respected the fact that he didn't equivocate. However, when the programmes were aired, the party issued a statement which read as follows, 'No such meeting took place as described. This is corroborated by indubitable evidence', and concluded, 'the timing of Dr Paisley's departure had been entirely a matter for him'.

Ahead of the broadcast of the trailers for the Paisley documentary, no one could have conceived of the breadth of vituperative recriminations coming from within the Paisley household. A DUP source told me after my documentaries went out, 'All our people were watching your programmes from behind the couch. No one knew what was coming next, but I can tell you one thing, when you named Timothy Johnston, a roar went up across Ulster.'

In advance of broadcasting the documentary, we gave the Paisleys an opportunity to watch the programmes. They didn't ask us to change one word, and the former moderator and DUP party leader only made one comment: 'You cannot undo history.'

From my first day in journalism in Northern Ireland, I had watched Paisley working incessantly to topple and wreck his political opponents and to undo any political structures that signalled accommodation of Dublin involvement. He was in every sense a wrecker, flirting and skirting with people who used unparliamentary language and bore all the hallmarks of militarism. This is why I found that breakfast in his home in 2006, when he told me that he wanted everyone working together before he expired, all the more remarkable. The proof of that pudding was that he delivered. This begs the argument – does it matter in reality what decided for him to act in that way at the end of his life. I think I err on the side of generosity towards him – whatever reservations I might have had about his reasons, I'm prepared to give him the benefit of the doubt. Interestingly, in a similar tone, former Prime Minister Tony Blair – who spent hours in Paisley's company – said of him, 'I felt this was a man looking into his own soul and feeling differently. He hadn't exactly matured, but he had in some indefinable sense broadened.'

Those days of recording Ian Paisley and his wife, Eileen, are memorable. The revelations that flowed from the documentaries filled news pages for over a week, and the programmes set new record viewing figures for BBC NI Current Affairs output. Being afforded an opportunity to capture on camera the life of one of Northern Ireland's most controversial politicians ever is right up there with the best stories I ever broke. The deposing of Paisley, firstly by the Free Presbyterian Church and then by the DUP, was even more ruthless and bloody than I'd ever imagined.

Ian Paisley and I had a good rapport from the first day I met him and that rapport continued until the very last day I spoke to him. He died on 12 September 2014 at the age of eighty-eight.

The fate of Paisley as a Church and political leader should serve as a lesson for all who would seek high office. Julius Caesar got it right: *Et tu, Brute.*

Chapter Twelve

Reflections on Irish Republicanism

IN THE MID-EIGHTIES, I co-authored a book on the Provisional IRA with Patrick Bishop, formerly of *The Observer*. We were writing and researching at a time when the Provisionals were escalating their campaign of violence resourced with state-of-the-art arms and weaponry supplied by Libya, including ground-to-air missiles. At that stage, the IRA was still a killing machine hiding behind a wall of secrecy. Death was the price to be paid by members, or indeed civilians, in the event of compromising IRA security through informing or otherwise. The finding of bodies along the Louth–South Armagh border was not uncommon in those days, and breaking through the IRA's wall of silence was challenging for investigative journalists and authors like me. The outworking of that reality was that the media and outside world simply did not know, for much of the time, what was going on in terms of IRA strategy and thinking. I always held to the view that 'nothing was ever what it seemed when it came to the IRA'.

For young soldiers from Manchester or Glasgow, even if they had been in South Armagh for 100 years, they would not understand why a field had been ploughed out of season, as actually happened – the purpose being to secretly run a wire beneath a furrow to trigger a roadside bomb. Ignorance of the IRA's modus operandi and intentions didn't stop there. More often than not, the security services had limited knowledge of what the IRA was doing – particularly, but not exclusively, in places like South Armagh. How, for example, did IRA activist Patrick Magee, months before the 1984 Conservative Party conference in Brighton, smuggle explosives undetected into the Grand Hotel in which Prime Minister Margaret Thatcher was going to sleep? Who was asleep on the job? How did the IRA manage to get close enough to Downing Street to launch a mortar-bomb attack in February 1991 while Prime Minister John Major and his ministerial colleagues were holding a Cabinet meeting?

This opaque world in which the IRA moved gave rise to mischief, misinformation and disinformation. I was suckered at times, as were other journalists. Much has been written about the IRA over the decades, but it is only now that their militant campaign is over that writers of history like myself are gradually seeing behind the screen what was actually happening in the theatre of war. For the greater part, the IRA's management cunningly concealed the stresses and strains within the many tiers of the organisation. An awful lot of the internal wrangling that occurred was among the upper echelons over pivoting from militancy to constitutionalism. This matter bedevilled the IRA from the early eighties, when Sinn Féin President Gerry Adams urged the Catholic Church to put in place an alternative strategy to endlessly condemning the IRA's militant campaign.

✳✳✳

Initially there was only one IRA, dating back to 1919. The original goal was to remove the British presence from Ireland – and then, after partition, it was to bring about a united Ireland. Between 1956 and 1962, the IRA carried out a militant border campaign, but in the late sixties chose to follow a more socialist, left-leaning non-military path in pursuance of a united Ireland. The words 'IRA – I Ran Away' were written in August 1969 on the Falls Road Public Baths owned by Belfast Corporation in reference to a decision by the IRA in the city to fall into line with the Dublin-based leadership to stand down the military arm of its organisation, choosing instead to pursue the goal of a united Ireland using strictly peaceful means. This policy gave rise to a split in republicanism in 1969 and the emergence of the Provisional IRA in Northern Ireland in 1970, which assumed the right to unilaterally act militarily on behalf of nationalists. The Official IRA, the remnants of the original organisation, declared a formal ceasefire in 1972, but what is interesting is the fact that two command areas, South Armagh and South Derry, did not allow themselves to be aligned to the Provisional IRA's GHQ until early 1977. Future Provisional IRA commander Martin McGuinness once told me that he initially joined what he called 'the wrong IRA' – the Official IRA.

As a young journalist in the eighties, while researching the book on the Provisional IRA, an old member of the Official IRA in Belfast, Jim Sullivan, told me that when the Troubles broke out in 1969, there were only eight guns to be found to defend nationalists at Catholic–Protestant flashpoints in the Lower Falls area of West Belfast. Dungannon priest Father Denis Faul told me the only man in Tyrone who knew where the guns were hidden was in jail for a non-political offence.

Someone had to go into the prison to find out where the guns were. When I interviewed South Derry solicitor Kevin Agnew, he had a similar story. He said there was only a handful of guns available to protect members of the People's Democracy, a student movement marching from Belfast to Derry in January 1969. A high-profile businessman from Andersonstown in West Belfast revealed to me how he drove as far south as Kerry, in the Republic of Ireland, in search of guns, fearful that Catholic areas were going to be invaded and overrun by angry loyalists.

The Provisionals gained credibility for their efforts to physically defend areas under attack by loyalists during riots in Belfast on the back of an overreaction by the Northern Ireland unionist-dominated government to protests by the civil rights movement. That movement was agitating for Catholics and nationalists to have a vote in local government elections, and the right to own a home and get a job on merit. One of the key drivers behind the Provisional IRA's more militant policy at that time was Belfast republican Joe Cahill, who would later become that organisation's chief of staff.

British soldiers were also dispatched to Northern Ireland in August 1969, ostensibly to protect nationalists under attack from loyalists. 'Operation Banner' was the name of the British armed forces' military operation. At first, the soldiers were welcomed by the Catholic community in West Belfast, but Cahill spoke to me about the two sides having 'a short-lived honeymoon'. In other words, the British military presence, coupled with the excesses of the RUC against nationalists, was soon being met with physical-force resistance from the Provisional IRA.

The Provisionals themselves would split in November 1986, when a majority of Sinn Féin voted during its Ard-Fheis to overturn the longstanding policy of abstentionism from the Irish parliament. This resulted in a former Sinn Féin president, Ruairí Ó Brádaigh, and Dáithí O'Conaill (both ex IRA chiefs of staff) and about thirty others walking out during Sinn Féin's annual conference in Dublin, the outcome of which was the founding of Republican Sinn Féin. I remember like yesterday following Ó Brádaigh and his dissenters to a hotel in West Dublin, where they held a press conference. Years later, while researching, I tracked down another republican veteran in the same hotel. That was Billy McKee, who by then was advancing in years. McKee was something of a legend in Belfast republicanism, credited with saving St Matthew's Catholic church on the Newtownards Road in East Belfast when it came under attack from loyalists at the outbreak of the Troubles. Stacking stout bottles in a dingy storeroom was a far cry from being a hero in Belfast. McKee looked and sounded miserable. When I asked him, 'Do you miss Belfast?', he said, 'It is lonely down here. I do miss Belfast.' When I asked him to do an interview he replied, 'I am not talking until the war is over.' That was the last time I saw McKee, who was an uncle of Seán Savage, one of the Gibraltar Three shot dead by the SAS in March 1988.

An IRA commander once told me, 'There were two constants at the heart of Provisional republicanism, "the Long War", and "making British establishment figures pay a price for supporting and financing the Army presence in Northern Ireland".' The philosophy of targeting the British establishment was drawn to the public's attention by the IRA in the wake of a no-warning bomb on 29 October 1975 at an Italian restaurant in Mayfair, London, which wounded eighteen people. The then chief of staff, Seamus Twomey, said, 'By hitting Mayfair restaurants, we were hitting the type of person that could bring pressure to bear on the British government.' Bringing the IRA's violent campaign to London would obtain right up to the Docklands bombing on 9 February 1996, which was effectively the last major IRA attack in Britain before the signing of the Good Friday Agreement on 10 April 1998. I was walking down Dawson Street in Dublin when a journalist colleague, David Davin-Power, phoned me to alert me to the attack. Channel 4 News called me almost immediately after that, and I contributed live to their programme from a TV studio opposite the Oireachtas.

The path to peace from 1969 to 1996 was painful for the British establishment. Earl Mountbatten (who regularly holidayed in Ireland), members of his family and Fermanagh teenager Paul Maxwell were killed at sea off the Mullaghmore Peninsula in County Sligo in August 1979 when the IRA triggered a remote-control bomb attached to Mountbatten's boat. Three days after the bombing, the IRA claimed responsibility, describing the attack as 'a discriminate act to bring to the attention of the English people the continuing occupation of our country'.

Then, in a remarkable breach of British security in October 1984, the IRA came within inches of wiping out Prime Minister Margaret Thatcher with a long-delay time bomb, which was planted in the Grand Hotel in Brighton by Patrick Magee a month before Thatcher and her Cabinet would arrive at the hotel for the Conservative Party conference. Though the prime minister escaped injury, five people were killed, including Deputy Chief Whip Anthony Berry MP. Thirty-one others were injured. The statement of admission for the Brighton Bombing was given to my colleague Deric Henderson, who in turn gave it to me. He often jokes that he expects that little piece of paper to come up for sale in Sotheby's with other Troubles memorabilia I own, but for the life of me I cannot find that quoin stone of history.

In 1990, Margaret Thatcher lost her close advisor Ian Gow in a car bombing. A further embarrassment for the British security services would follow on 7 February 1991, when the IRA carried out a mortar-bomb attack on Downing Street, just three years before the 1994 IRA cessation of violence. This was an attempt to assassinate Prime Minister John Major and his War Cabinet, who were meeting to discuss the Gulf War. Despite the escalation in IRA activity and the attendant propaganda value, that organisation had reached a conclusion – as had Colonel James Glover, the highest-ranking officer in the British Army – that neither side could win. Reflecting on the reality that the IRA could not ultimately defeat a superior force like the British Army, a former IRA strategist told me recently, 'there was a growing realisation we were engaged in a war of attrition and in any war of attrition the bigger side will always prevail in the long-term. In guerrilla warfare there are two imperatives: for the State, the imperative is to crush the insurgency, and for the guerrilla forces, to survive militarily until the conditions, for a negotiated settlement become possible'. English radical and IRA activist Rose Dugdale, whom I met once, opined, 'Success for the IRA resided in its "surviving militarily" until those conditions for a negotiated settlement fell into place.'

In a leaked UK Ministry of Defence document of 1979, which fell into the IRA's hands, titled 'Future Terrorist Trends' and written by General James Glover when he was BGS (Int)

(Brigadier General Staff, Intelligence), it was highlighted that 'the IRA had taken a calculated decision to regroup from their earlier position of weakness. It now had a new and effective cellular structure, and was equipped with all the sinews of war – men, money and weapons – and must be taken seriously.' Glover, in an interview with Peter Taylor in 1988 on the BBC's *Panorama*, when asked if he thought the IRA could be defeated, said, 'In no way can or will the Provisional Irish Republican Army ever be defeated militarily.' In a briefing to journalists in November 1989, 100 days into office, NI Secretary of State Peter Brooke, answering a question from the Press Association's Deric Henderson about the chances of defeating the IRA, said, 'It is difficult to envisage a military defeat of such a force because of the circumstances under which they operate.' The best that the police and army could do, he said, was to contain the violence to 'enable normal life to go on'.

In fact, a high-ranking IRA figure active in the late eighties told me that by 1988 the IRA was beginning to look towards 'The Endgame'. Regardless, its campaign of bombing and killing would continue for another eight years, but, unknown to the outside world, in the mid-eighties Sinn Féin President Gerry Adams persuaded Father Alec Reid of Clonard Monastery in West Belfast to try to convince the former Irish taoiseach and Fianna Fáil leader Charles Haughey to meet with him and Sinn Féin. This resulted in SDLP leader John Hume accepting Haughey's suggestion that he ought to engage with Adams directly while keeping him in the loop. With political nationalism on the island of Ireland starting to knit together, this made space for negotiations that eventually involved the Sinn Féin leadership. The foundations were being laid for republicanism to espouse constitutional politics, full stop – although there were many bends on the road to the cessation of the IRA's militant campaign on 31 August 1994.

***

I now know that throughout 1993 there was a palpable tension within the IRA. Many insiders were blindsided by the exposure of secret lines of communication between the IRA and the British government, which I disclosed that November. These behind-the-scenes political moves resulted in stirrings in the IRA ranks. There were even suspicions at the highest level of the IRA that 'a small number of people were secreting guns'. The chief of staff became aware that the quartermaster general, Michael McKevitt, who had oversight of all arms caches, was implying that he didn't trust the 'army lines, the logistical sinews, dumps, staging houses, and supply chains'. McKevitt made it known he intended to retain around 20 per cent of all the supplies coming into the country, which he intended to distribute himself. An IRA commander said, 'It was clear to me the Quartermaster General was preparing for a breakaway.' It was feared that there might be a challenge to the IRA leadership.

Apparently, when the full extent of what had been going on below the radar revealed itself in 1994, Michael McKevitt ran the risk of 'execution' for treachery and misuse of matériel belonging to the IRA. This did not come to pass because the IRA leadership feared an internal backlash against any such move.

A pre-1994 IRA ceasefire internal document had been drafted and circulated at the highest levels in the republican movement. This paper was something of a curate's egg, with different people free to interpret it in whatever way they chose. The document, commonly referred to as TUAS, fell into my hands courtesy of the DUP's Reverend William McCrea MP. It is now known that TUAS was the work not of one person but of several key individuals. It was informed by a need for 'ambivalence' because the IRA's 1994 cessation would come with a series of internal and external differences over closure to the 'armed struggle', so the ambiguity arising from the acronym was a very deliberate tactic of its authors. I readily admit my interpretation of TUAS at the time was ill-informed and wrong. I now know that it was to be read internally as a 'Tactical Use of Armed Struggle', but externally it was to be interpreted as a 'Totally UnArmed Strategy'. The Totally UnArmed Strategy meaning was sold to Irish America and the Dublin government, while IRA members were being briefed that its army was maintaining the capacity to tactically deploy military action as and when necessary. I, too, bought into the Totally UnArmed Strategy interpretation, and I apologise for getting that wrong.

A meeting of republicans from all over the island of Ireland took place in Letterkenny in Donegal on 24 July 1994. When I arrived in the car park at the hotel where republicans had assembled, I was approached by a very senior figure who advised me that 'every IRA unit on the island of Ireland had been consulted and the Reynolds–Major Agreement was rejected', adding, 'but be careful ... there could be a silver lining'. I went live on RTÉ Radio immediately to report what I had just heard. The reference to 'a silver lining' left me puzzled, but I now know that the subliminal message being conveyed to me was that even though the IRA had rejected the Downing Street Declaration, the Sinn Féin leadership was being afforded some space to further engage the British and Irish governments to firm up the substance of the Hume–Adams document seen by republicans as a basis for going forward politically.

A dissenting voice in the IRA in 1993 had explained to me why he was against the Downing Street Declaration. He stated, 'it reiterated a version of consent which gifted unionism a veto on practically everything'. He contended it also committed the Irish government to a de facto recognition of British sovereignty over the Six Counties in committing to remove Articles 2 and 3 from the Irish Constitution. In essence, this was viewed as a setting aside of the Republic of Ireland's constitutional claim over Northern Ireland. He added, 'While Hume–Adams was always constant about the right of the people of the island of Ireland to decide on the issue of self-determination, without external impediment, the idea that a Northern Ireland secretary of state should be the arbiter as to when a border poll should take place was anathema to some senior IRA personnel.' The SDLP's Mark Durkan clarified for me: 'The reason why this matter was left in the hands of a secretary of state, on whom there was an obligation to call a border poll if it were clear the circumstances had arrived, was because the parties could not politically agree criteria for or when a border poll should be called.'

Despite there being some unionist scepticism, both communities in Northern Ireland breathed a sigh of relief when the IRA called a cessation to violence on 31 August 1994. An insider described this action as 'the most popular thing the IRA ever did', but all was not well inside the IRA with so much uncertainty about republican gains flowing from its unilateral decision. There were tensions within the command structure, with people at one management level feeling they were not being adequately kept abreast by another command level. Those stresses in the IRA hierarchy were further exacerbated by endless demands from London and unionism to use the word 'permanent' about the cessation. The spat that developed over the necessity for IRA decommissioning before talks added to tension in the republican camp. Prime Minster Major's dependence for survival on Unionist MPs at Westminster effectively tied his hands from moving swiftly to the next stage of bedding down the recently born peace. The Major government was also refusing to engage Sinn Féin. I recall meeting Nelson Mandela in Washington around that time and asking him, 'Do you think John Major should be talking to republicans?' His response was unambiguous: 'There has to be talks. Talks are the only way ahead.'

Politics appeared to continue to trigger unrest within IRA ranks. Throughout 1995, there were endless internal arguments at Army Council level. In autumn 1995, a senior republican spoke of 'a big angry black dog running around'. John Major was now a lame-duck prime minister, his power ebbing away. I concluded back then that the IRA cessation would not hold. Soon, it would be clear the post-cessation phase of the Peace Process was 'at an end'. This message was conveyed to a select number of key figures in the IRA. An instruction was given to the chief of staff to be ready and prepared to carry out 'a spectacular' in England. The outworking of this was the 9 February 1996 Docklands bombing in London. The last IRA bombing in Britain took place on 26 March 1997, when a rail track near Wilmslow, Cheshire, was targeted. No one was hurt. There was a simultaneous scare at Doncaster.

In September 1996, an IRA convention took place – followed by another in 1997. After the second convention, a number of people left the organisation. It is reckoned that about 5 per cent went to the Real IRA; 2 per cent reportedly simply went home. An IRA source said that between 1998 and 2005 over 80 per cent of frontline IRA members left as individuals, reportedly disheartened by the process and less than enamoured by what appeared to be Sinn Féin's appeasement of intransigent unionism, which was deemed unwilling to engage in the Peace Process, with its calls for assurance on permanence of the IRA cessation and topped off by DUP leader Ian Paisley's demand for the IRA 'to wear sackcloth and ashes' to show repentance. What continues to baffle me is how the Sinn Féin leadership, ostensibly Gerry Adams and Martin McGuinness, ever managed to convince the IRA to call a cessation, given the endless turmoil in its ranks.

The arrival in Downing Street on 2 May 1997 of Tony Blair, supported in Northern Ireland by Secretary of State Mo Mowlam, meant that the dial on the clock of Irish history was about to move. Through the good offices of Mowlam, in an interview with the BBC's late political correspondent Jim Dougal, Blair sent a signal ahead of taking office that the door to talks would open to Sinn Féin should IRA violence cease. Once engaged in what became known as the Good Friday negotiations with the political parties, including Sinn Féin, Blair involved his Dublin counterpart, Bertie Ahern, elected taoiseach in June 1997. Furthermore, he deepened American involvement, already represented by Senator George Mitchell and President Bill Clinton. This proved pivotal, particularly in the case of Trimble, who was fighting a losing battle inside his own party about going into government with Sinn Féin before IRA decommissioning had commenced. A 'concocted' British government side letter pledging serious action against Sinn Féin after six months in the event of the IRA failing to put arms beyond use, coupled with a personal phone call from President Clinton, empowered Trimble to sign the Good Friday Agreement. History had been made. Canadian General John de Chastelain – who led the international, independent commission on decommissioning, which oversaw the destruction of weapons – said on 26 September 2005, 'we are satisfied that the arms decommissioned represent the totality of the IRA's arsenal'.

Do I believe the Catholic nationalist community will ever find itself as defenceless as it found itself in 1969 if it were to come under attack in the future? I do not. The term 'putting arms beyond use' is a wonderfully Jesuitical term. Would it be possible for any future organisation like the IRA to carry on a similar violent campaign over such a sustained period? It is difficult to imagine that.

Technology now in the hands of governments for the purposes of surveillance and monitoring the movement of people is so sophisticated that the use of guerrilla warfare would no longer be enough. Even before these technological advancements, when the IRA had some of the most sophisticated weaponry in the world courtesy of Libya by the late eighties, activists found themselves unable to remove heavy weaponry after attacks. The escalation in the IRA's border campaign in that decade resulted in the British government putting more resources into not just personnel on the ground, but also surveillance. This resulted in the IRA's biggest loss of personnel on 8 May 1987, when the East Tyrone Brigade undertook a full-frontal assault on an RUC base with a digger, a bomb and heavy weapons. The target was the Loughgall village police station in Armagh, close to the Irish border. Unknown to the elite eight-man IRA squad, the SAS was lying in wait and killed all eight men and a civilian called Anthony Hughes who drove into the ambush. That was a costly learning experience and it wasn't lost on the IRA's long-term thinking.

Moreover, in all the militant and political campaigns in which Ireland has been involved, Irish America has been, morally, psychologically and monetarily important. The American Noraid was one organisation that proved critical when it came to raising funds for republicanism during the Troubles in Northern Ireland. Could any republican organisation, engaging in a violent campaign on the island of Ireland today – post-9/11, and given what Russia is currently doing in Ukraine – expect US dollars to flow across the Atlantic for the purpose of killing in Northern Ireland? Not a chance, in my opinion. It is a new world.

In one of the last conversations I had with the late Martin McGuinness in his home in Derry, we spoke man to man. I was unequivocal in telling him that coming from where I came, with a Catholic upbringing and a sense of duty of care to all, without exception, I could not square using violence to kill another human being for political reasons. He stared at me and asked, 'How do you think I feel?' It was quite a moment. I asked the Sinn Féin vice president on another occasion, 'How many police officers or soldiers did you kill?' Those piercing blue eyes stared through me and a voice answered, 'I've never told anybody that.' He also told me years ago that in 1972, when William Whitelaw, the Northern Ireland secretary of state, arranged for an IRA delegation to fly to Cheyne Walk in London for talks, he was, in

IRA parlance, 'packing': concealing a gun on his person. When I inquired about the wisdom of this and the dangers attached to being caught in possession of a weapon, the former deputy first minister told me, 'If any of us were going down, so were some of them.'

In conversation with another republican who had killed a police officer, I asked him, 'How could you shoot him dead in cold blood?' 'I only saw the uniform,' he said. Had I been incurious, I would not have asked the questions I posed about the taking of life by members of the IRA or loyalists. Discussing this matter with a former senior IRA activist, he startled me in saying, 'You have to kill a fair amount of your own humanity when you are engaged in conflict. You have to diminish the humanity of those targeted to the status of targets. You can't see their humanity.'

Is it conceivable that an IRA campaign of violence as we knew it for over a quarter of a century might be replicated? I put this question to a former senior member of the IRA. His response was the following. The advances in technology in the hands of government preclude any sustainable IRA campaign of violence. There is no credible nationalist grievance that could sustain it. The capacity built up by the IRA was sufficient to bring about a mutual desire to deliver a political settlement, and even if that capacity, which rested in the hands of the IRA, obtained today, the nationalist community would not support another violent campaign. Republicanism also needed American support in many measures, but 9/11 changed all that.

So it seems clear to me that the notion of any IRA ever returning to the campaign of violence as we knew it is dead in the water.

Chapter Thirteen

History in the Making

I CHOSE TO BE a journalist, not a political activist or politician. That said, coming from the background that I have detailed in the early chapters of this book, it should be understandable why I would not espouse a political party in government which legislates in favour of the better-off in society.

When I describe myself as 'intellectually to the left', I mean my empathy emotionally rests with the less well-off, not just locally but globally. As a non-political-party activist in Northern Ireland, I am restricted in my ability to effect change. In a personal capacity, we sent our children to State schools, post-primary, and any examination of how we addressed the issue of living in a divided society will show that when we needed people to help in a myriad of ways in our home, we deliberately gave that work to a non-Catholic. It was one of the concrete ways in which Detta and I have always tried to reach out to the other community.

I am not a royalist, but I have no hostility towards the British royal family. Furthermore, I could have chosen not to live in Northern Ireland, not to walk under the Union flag on Parliament Buildings, not to stand where 'God Save The

Queen' was being played – but, not being iconoclastic, I live and let live.

***

The Queen and her family didn't impinge on or impact our lives as a family growing up in South Armagh. It has to be remembered that during our childhood, we had no television; no glossy *Hello*-style magazines came into our house on a weekly or fortnightly basis. *The Far East, Secrets, Our Boys* and comics such as *The Beano, The Dandy* and *The Hotspur* would have been read in our house when we were children. We didn't see any flashy images nightly on a screen of Princess Margaret, other members of the royal family, or the Queen heading for Balmoral on their summer holidays. That situation remained the same right up until my going to university in 1970, when my parents moved to live at Creggan near Crossmaglen; only then did they get a television.

While royalty didn't register in our home, I discovered in Detta's landowning family in Galway a lingering cursory touch of the forelock in the direction of an earlier, British era of influence in Ireland. When I visited her uncle, Canon Paddy Costelloe, the parish priest of Headford in Co. Galway, in the early 1980s, he had the Union flag in the corner of his living room in the parochial house. A European and a linguist, he held to the view that Ireland should have remained in the Commonwealth.

When Detta and I got married and settled in Belfast, our two girls, Ciara and Laura-Kate, grew up in what one might call the 'era' of Princess Diana. Of course, the advent of TVAM opened a window onto all the glamour of the young princess, and to her world and her 'fairytale prince'. For that generation of children, this was real. They could watch all this live in their own breakfast rooms every morning. Detta and the children loved all this, but I remained somewhat detached from royal matters, and at no time did I ever express opinions about them in the course of my duty.

Interestingly, as a reporter at Downtown Radio from 1976 until the day I decided to walk away from the place, I only covered two royal visits. Perhaps that was a coincidence, but perhaps it was more by design because, being radical, I did not accept the protocol of not being free to put a question to anybody in public life – and I suspect the bosses in the Downtown newsroom feared I would violate the archaic, anachronistic protocol of not holding members of the royal family to account. Perhaps people still don't realise the media are forbidden to familiarise with royalty or question a member of the royal family in the course of journalistic duty.

I always loved breaking rules. I was not a rule-follower. I was the Harvey Smith of the broadcasting world in Northern Ireland. I once came into contact with Smith during the Dublin Horse Show, which I used to cover when I did a weekly farming programme for Downtown. I managed to get into the so-called 'pocket' arena, where I was hoping to corner him for an interview. Just then, an official spotted me and moved immediately to try to chuck me out of the enclosure. Smith, witnessing this, called out to me, 'Come here lad.' He directed me into a small hall, banged the door shut and said, 'What's he going to do now?' He proceeded to invite me to ask him what I wanted to know. 'Two Fingers Harvey' came good for me.

On another occasion, I turned up when Princess Diana

was visiting a charity in South Belfast. It was the day the Gulf War ended – 28 February 1991. As she left the building, I asked the question: 'Do you have any response to the ending of the Gulf War?' It was a soft-ball question, but, nevertheless, it was breaking protocol. Looking over at me, flashing those big doe eyes, she responded, 'Of course I am delighted, like everybody else.'

My second royal encounter was more substantive. It involved Prince, now King, Charles. He had been on a visit to Northern Ireland and went to police headquarters at Knock. I turned up in time to catch him bidding farewell to the chief constable and other senior officers. I fired a question at Charles to the effect of 'What about all these stories in the tabloid press about your private life?' He was obviously taken aback. It looked as if he was suddenly coming up for air. I doubt if any reporter had ever confronted him before the cameras on this matter.

Fortuitously for Charles, there was a UTV soundman called Jim McGirr there, who was carrying a boom mic – 8–10 feet long and commonly called 'a hairy dog' or 'a dead cat'. The boom mic was always held high above the fray. Prince Charles, buying time to come up with a response to my question, looked up at the mic and asked Jim, 'Are you fishing for something up there?' When he looked back at me, I repeated my question: 'What about all these allegations about your private life in the tabloid press?' 'You must not believe everything you read in the newspapers,' he replied.

Those were my only two close encounters with members of the royal family. Needless to say, I hadn't endeared myself to the NIO press officers, nor to the people accompanying Prince Charles. Today, now that Charles is king, I would potentially end up in the 'Camera stellata', or Star Chamber, guilty of insubordination!

***

In 2011, news broke that Queen Elizabeth had been invited by President Mary McAleese to visit the Irish Republic. The last British monarch to set foot in Ireland had been Queen Elizabeth's grandfather, King George V, who had made a coronation trip to Dublin 100 years earlier, when the whole of the island of Ireland was still a part of the United Kingdom.

The Queen had every reason not to visit Ireland against a historical and contemporary backdrop of hurt and grief visited upon her fellow countrymen and family. In 1921, King George V visited Belfast to address the State opening of the Northern Ireland parliament. The 10th Royal Hussars had travelled to Belfast from the Curragh in Kildare to escort the king during his time in Belfast. About ten miles away from where I was reared, at a place known locally in South Armagh as 'Francie's Bridge', as the Hussars' troop train with 113 men and 104 horses aboard was making its way back to the Curragh, a mine planted on the line by the IRA's Fourth Northern Division was triggered. The train was derailed, leading to the deaths of three members of the machine-gun troop, a railway guard and over forty horses. Michael Boyle from Cloughogue, uncle to my sister-in-law, Alice, was one of the local men called upon to bury the horses close to the railway line where they were blown up.

The folk memory of that South Armagh border-crossing assault on the king's horses reared its head again on 20 July 1982 in the wake of the IRA bombing of Hyde Park, in which some of the Queen's horses were killed. One of the horses which was seriously wounded, called Sefton, survived and became a bit of a celebrity.

The Queen had another reason for questioning the wisdom of visiting the Republic of Ireland. On 27 August 1979, Earl Mountbatten, her cousin and uncle of Prince Philip, was blown up with two members of his family and Enniskillen boy Paul Maxwell in the earl's fishing boat in Donegal Bay, off Mullaghmore in County Sligo. Undoubtedly, those deaths would have left a deep impression on the Queen and her husband.

I remember racing to Mullaghmore that August day. I couldn't get over the calmness of the water and the funereal silence in the picturesque village, which enjoys one of the greatest sea views anywhere in Ireland. The grotesqueness of the boat-bomb killings was in marked contrast to the quietude all around me.

On the evening of the day that the Mountbatten boat was bombed and eighteen British soldiers were killed in the Narrow Water ambush at Warrenpoint in South Down, 1,500 miles away, in the Vatican, the head of the Catholic Church in Ireland, Cardinal Tomás Ó Fiaich, known to me since boyhood, was meeting the pope's chief foreign-travel organiser, Archbishop Marcinkus. They were arranging a papal visit to Armagh city, the ecclesiastic centre in Ireland of both the Catholic Church and the Church of Ireland. Dr Ó Fiaich told me that by the end of the day he had learned from clergy back home that 'the atmosphere had been poisoned', rendering the first papal visit to Northern Ireland impossible in the circumstances.

The cardinal had agreed to meet the pope the next morning. He said he was shattered. 'When I explained the nuances militating against the pope going to Armagh, the head of the

Catholic Church responded: "Is it not all the more important now that I go?'" Summing up his sense of disappointment at the IRA's destruction of the prospect of the pope visiting Northern Ireland, the cardinal told me: 'It was just like Armagh having won the All-Ireland and as captain of the team and I was making my way up to the Hogan Stand to pick up [the] Sam Maguire and I collapsed.'

***

The treatment meted out to the Queen's family and soldiers by militant Irish activists over the decades continues to be set against the role played by members of the British Army, who were guilty of many atrocities during the Troubles in Northern Ireland. The Queen was the commander-in-chief of the UK's armed forces, including the Parachute Regiment. Members of that regiment were directly linked to the killings in Ballymurphy in West Belfast of at least nine innocent people between 9 and 11 August 1971. Again, on Bloody Sunday in Derry on 30 January 1972, the 1st Battalion of the Parachute Regiment was involved in the shooting of twenty-six unarmed civilians, thirteen of whom died immediately with another person dying as a result of the attack four months later.

However, despite conflicts between them, Ireland and Britain have changed and relationships between the two countries are much healthier today, in spite of how divisive Brexit has been. In recent times, the royal family has played its part in contributing to those improved relationships.

Ahead of writing this book, I knew little of the background to the Queen's State visit to the Irish Republic in May 2011.

By that stage, Northern Ireland was bedding down following on from the 1998 Good Friday Agreement, and Taoiseach Bertie Ahern was at the heart of this process. He made a major contribution, working hand in hand with British Prime Minister Tony Blair to create a much-improved relationship between Belfast, London and Dublin. However, Ahern did not survive as taoiseach to facilitate the Queen's visit to Dublin in 2011. By then, Enda Kenny, leader of Fine Gael, had taken on that role.

Mary McAleese was a power in the land in those days as president of Ireland. She was born in Ardoyne in North Belfast in Northern Ireland and had an insight into life there and in the Republic of Ireland. Interestingly, during her tenure as president there was no rapport whatsoever between her and me. When she visited the Royal Agriculture Show at Balmoral in South Belfast, I even put a question to her in Irish to humour her, aware that she speaks the language very well, but she chose to ignore me. The irony of the situation is that in recent times the former president was a guest on my UTV series *Eamonn Mallie: Face to Face with ...* and the interview was considered one of the most revealing and interesting she ever gave. She was the quintessence of civility and courtesy, both in front of the camera and to my producer, Michael; to my wife, Detta, who was present; and to the camera crew.

While I was not entirely interested in the royal visit to Ireland, what caught my attention at the time was the thoroughness of the healing agenda set out in the planning, which was then ruthlessly implemented by the royal visitor during her visit. The thought that went into the Queen's speech in Dublin Castle on 18 May was breathtaking.

The setting that night in Dublin Castle comprised a 'who's who' of Irish society, including Northern Ireland's first minister, Peter Robinson, and his wife, Iris, wearing an appropriate green dress. The Robinsons had just come through a very tumultuous domestic upheaval, and this was their first outing in public to a major event. One of the standout moments of that evening for me was when President McAleese hugged Iris Robinson in the most endearing fashion imaginable. It didn't appear to me that much was said, but the gesture spoke volumes. President McAleese embraced Iris with all the warmth and empathy of a sister. It was a manifestation of true humanity and showed an understanding of pain.

When the Queen stood up to speak in the presence of the president, the leadership of the Irish government, captains and kings of industry, and representatives of the arts, of women's organisations and the many professions in the Irish Republic and uttered the words 'A Uachtaráin, agus a chairde', to me it was truly a history-making moment in the vein of John F. Kennedy's 1963 comment in Berlin, 'Ich bin ein Berliner.'

The following comment by Queen Elizabeth also caught me, and I am sure her audience, by surprise. She said, 'With the benefit of historical hindsight we can all see things which we wish had been done differently or not at all. But it is also true that no one who looked to the future over the past centuries could have imagined the strength of the bonds that are now in place between the governments and the people of our two nations, the spirit of partnership that we now enjoy, and the lasting rapport between us.'

Rarely in my professional career have I ever responded to and thought so deeply about the content of a speech as that delivered by the Queen in Dublin. In opening her address *as Gaeilge* in front of the people of Ireland, after all the centuries of struggle between the British and the Irish, she was closing the door on the past, acknowledging the validity of Ireland as a nation and showing respect for its mother tongue.

I continue to be excited about that moment in time. What surprises me is the limited attention historians have given to the messages peppered throughout the speech, which were profound, challenging, historic and forward-looking. This was a more perspicacious address than I had ever heard falling from the lips of any British politician when addressing Irish–British matters. This was a departure on a grand scale from so many of the mealy-mouthed utterances of British politicians down the decades. I only wish I had my life to live again to embark on a doctorate where I could place the Queen's speech in the proper context of great speeches of our time. For someone like myself, who had little or no interest in royalty, here was an occasion when a member of that family shone a light into a corner which no British individual had ever done before.

The Queen, however, didn't stop at making that historic speech in Dublin Castle. Thanks to Mary McAleese, who sat literally inches away from her when she delivered that seminal address, we can now get a fuller insight into the planning of the extraordinary events in which the Queen allowed herself to become involved during her visit to Dublin. The former president, in her very considerable tome *Here's the Story*, outlines some of the thinking behind the choice of venues visited during the Queen's visit to Dublin. She has graciously empowered me to draw on her text to flesh out my exposition on the royal visit to the Irish Republic and to Northern Ireland.

The former president and her husband, Martin, spent much of their tenure in office building bridges to loyalist/unionist organisations in Northern Ireland. Clearly, President McAleese empathised with the Queen on many fronts – and it is evident from reading her book that the Queen genuinely liked the Ardoyne-born woman and believed in her as a human being who desired to heal and bring people together. The fact that President McAleese had joined the monarch on a visit to the Island of Ireland Peace Park at Messines in Belgium stood her in good stead in persuading her to visit Ireland. A pledge by President McAleese to the Queen's officials that she intended to accompany her on her visit to the Great War memorial at Islandbridge in Dublin was also a mature and smart move.

In planning the Queen's visit, Mary McAleese said she suggested three things to Edward Young, the deputy private secretary to the Queen. The first was the laying of a wreath at the Garden of Remembrance in Parnell Square in Dublin, which commemorates all those who fought for Irish freedom over the centuries. She argued that to do this early in the visit would silence the begrudgers and 'soften' a lot of hardened hearts; that it would, without words or elaboration, put the healing of history's wounds right at the very top of the Queen's agenda. The second suggestion was a visit to Croke Park, the home of the Gaelic Athletic Association. President McAleese explained to Young that the GAA is a major community-based success story and that she wanted Queen Elizabeth to see the best of the Irish people. Third, she suggested that the Queen should speak a few words in Irish, contending that it would carry major significance.

Shrewdly, during a meeting with British Ambassador Francis Campbell, who is from Newry, President McAleese scribbled a greeting in Irish on a piece of paper for potential use. She then sat in awe when the Queen opened her address in fluent Irish, greeting her and the guests, 'A Uachtaráin, agus a chairde ...' What was not insignificant on that particular evening was the fact that Ireland's best-known poet, Seamus Heaney, sat only a few seats away, participating in a royal toast. Heaney had travelled a long way too, as we reflect on the words he wrote some years prior to 2011: 'Be advised, my passport's green. No glass of ours was ever raised to toast the Queen.'

Had I been asked ahead of the Queen's visit to Dublin, 'Are the following venues and events potential runners in which to involve the Queen?', I would have opined that the laying of a wreath in the Garden of Remembrance in Parnell Square in Dublin was 'out', a visit to Croke Park was 'out' and the Queen speaking Irish was 'out' – but looking back, history would have laughed at me.

***

The Hogan Stand in Croke Park, built in 1924, has, as explained by Mary McAleese, a deep historical resonance for GAA lovers arising from the killing of Tipperary county footballer Michael Hogan and thirteen spectators by British forces on 21 November 1920. The assault by the British has been historically linked to the IRA's killing of fourteen people in a series of coordinated attacks across Dublin with the aim of assassinating alleged British Intelligence agents or spies.

That same Hogan Stand was to the forefront of people's minds in 2007 when, for the first time ever, a game of rugby was played in Croke Park between Ireland and England – the old enemy. I am starting to well up as I write of that famous day. In the sixty-fourth minute, Shane Horgan, a former Meath GAA minor footballer, climbed up into the clouds, seized a cross-field kick from Ronan O'Gara and scored a try for Ireland, changing its fortunes and beating England for the third time in a row – and, above all, in Croke Park.

No sooner had the final whistle blown than my phone rang. Detta and I and the children had been watching the game in a hotel in Morzine in France, where we had been skiing. My great and dear friend Jim Aiken, who was dying with cancer in his South Belfast home, was at the other end of the line telling me, 'Eamonn, it's a great day for the people of Ireland, for all the people of Ireland.' Those were Jim's last words to me. We had to cut short our ski trip to return to Belfast for his funeral. *Suaimhneas síoraí d'anam*, Jim.

That moment, that day in Croke Park, like the day that Michael Hogan was shot dead in 1920, will live forever wherever that Ireland–England game of rugby is discussed.

✳ ✳ ✳

In her autobiography, Mary McAleese spells out how she saw all of the gestures by the Queen as a great opportunity for genuine healing to take place between Ireland and Britain. As a result of good guidance and judgement from Sir Christopher Geidt, her Private Secretary, the Queen appreciated the wisdom proffered. She obviously valued the genuineness of President McAleese's 'bridge-building' efforts.

Perhaps one fact eluded Mary McAleese about the Queen, although in fairness she usually knows her facts. In 1937, when the late Queen was eleven years old, she and Princess Margaret spent their summer holiday in Rostrevor in South Down. They came there to stay with their aunt, one of the Bowes-Lyon family, who owned Kilbroney Estate. In fact, folksinger Tommy Sands owns the stables which used to belong to the Bowes-Lyon family. They butt onto his home.

The Queen revealed her ongoing affection for Rostrevor and Warrenpoint in the early eighties in the most unusual of circumstances. The head of the Fire Service in South Down, Eamonn Magee, was decorated at Buckingham Palace for his services to his community, with particular reference to the actions of him and his team at the time of the IRA killing of eighteen soldiers in a double bombing in August 1979 at Narrow Water Castle near Warrenpoint.

Tommy Sands and Magee had been at school together and had both been altar servers in the local church in Mayobridge. After Magee received his royal honour, Sands, a regular broadcaster for many years on Downtown Radio, caught up with him. His old school friend shared with Sands his experience with the Queen when receiving his award. Sands was fascinated with his account of that exchange. Being the professional that he is, Sands committed Magee's story to tape and kindly let me listen to the recording. The late Magee explained how the Queen warmed to him immediately when they met in Buckingham Palace. She set about telling him about her time in Rostrevor as a young girl and of how she enjoyed running about in the Mournes. According to Sands' recording of Magee's conversation with the Queen, she took him by the surprise when she asked, 'How are they all at the 'Point?' Magee could not get over her use of the colloquialism when speaking about Warrenpoint.

His host told him she had seen her first 'moving' picture on a screen in a cinema in Warrenpoint. The Queen had a greater personal connectedness to this island than many realise.

***

Sinn Féin clearly realised they had made a huge misjudgement in not being present at Dublin Castle in 2011 during Queen Elizabeth's State visit. What they had failed to take into consideration was the fact that the world had changed, that the new generation was very much governed by what it saw on breakfast TV and in glossy magazines, which habitually promoted the image of the new royals, particularly inspired by the era of Princess Diana. Young Irish people weren't so preoccupied with the history and differences that obtained between these islands over old wounds and wars. *Hello* magazine, and images of Diana in her latest dress, meant much more to this generation. They were not hidebound by old shibboleths and innate prejudices. The Queen too had moved with the times. Sinn Féin had come to realise that hubris had been a burden on its own development.

Martin McGuinness was determined that when the next opportunity arose, he would put to right that deficit. In fact, in an interview with Jeremy Paxman on the BBC, McGuinness, speaking of the Queen's visit in 2011, said, 'I watched the conduct of that visit very carefully and I have to say I was tremendously impressed, tremendously impressed that Queen Elizabeth was prepared to stand in solemn commemoration of those people who fought against British rule in Ireland – that she was prepared to honour the Irish language the way that she did.'

When word got out about the possibility of a handshake between Martin McGuinness (the former IRA number two in Derry, as revealed by himself during the Saville Inquiry into the events of Bloody Sunday), I heard people saying, 'The country's cowped', a Norse/Ulster-Scots expression meaning 'the world is upside down' or, in this instance, 'this cannot be happening'. But fact is often stranger than fiction. In 2012, the Queen was scheduled to undertake a tour of England, Scotland, Wales and Northern Ireland to mark her Diamond Jubilee, it being the sixtieth anniversary of her accession. Privately, those close to Deputy First Minister McGuinness knew he had realised, on the back of the Good Friday Agreement and the success of the royal visit in 2011, that the time had come to make a gesture. According to insiders, it was he who initiated the meeting with the Queen ahead of her visit to Northern Ireland.

The royal household, when alerted to the McGuinness proposition, was said to find it very acceptable. That whole visit, however, had the potential to be tricky and even dangerous for both parties. Those planning the Queen's visit and the handshake with McGuinness had to be mindful of many eventualities. McGuinness had to be aware of the thinking of his base, of the views of his party leadership and of former IRA members who had lain in jail for years, some of whom had gone on hunger strike or had watched their friends either dying on hunger strike or being killed by loyalists or the Queen's State forces. The folk memory in republicanism is a lethal instrument. Furthermore, dissident republicans, driven by hubris, the same hubris that once held Martin McGuinness and his generation of republicans captive, have not gone away.

The task of putting in place arrangements for a handshake

between the Queen and McGuinness fell to Leo Green, Sinn Féin's political director at Stormont. Green was a former hunger striker who had spent seventeen years in jail for killing a police officer. His role entailed liaising with Julian King, the director general of the NIO, in the first instance, configuring the dynamics of any coming together of the Queen and the deputy first minister. King, in turn, liaised with Sir Christopher Geidt. The royal household had readily bought into the suggestion that McGuinness and the Queen should meet and shake hands, seeing the merit and the potential for healing Anglo-Irish relations, and Geidt displayed no reticence in running with this proposition. At a later stage, Vincent Parker, who was special advisor to McGuinness, became directly involved with Green and King.

Behind the scenes, as preparations were taking shape for this unprecedented meeting, the republican leadership was doing its homework, assessing and evaluating the potential downside of a meeting – not to mention a handshake – between McGuinness and the Queen. A committee was established at the highest level of the republican movement to undertake an audit of all risks, the ups, the downs and the positives which might flow from such a handshake. Heading up that committee were Bobby Storey, Martin Lynch and Ted Howell, three of the most powerful individuals in the republican movement. They were determined to keep a tight grip on every move.

The one thing that Martin McGuinness could not risk was to be seen shaking hands with the Queen in front of thousands of unionists waving Union Jacks at Hillsborough Castle. Initially, a plan had been drawn up to hold the meeting and handshake involving the Queen, First Minister Peter Robinson and Martin

McGuinness on the steps of Parliament Buildings in Stormont in front of at least 10,000 people. Plans were being made to invite them to assemble in the grounds of Stormont Estate. This would have involved a major undertaking and the putting in place of a very considerable infrastructure – including barricades, crowd-control barriers and toilets – to facilitate such a large crowd. Not only would the NIO have had to issue invitations to its own guests, but councils across Northern Ireland would also have had to be afforded an opportunity to send a representative spread of people from the various areas. It was anticipated that up to 15,000 people would have been present on the day.

The security services were of the opinion that this would be too challenging. Hillsborough Castle grounds had been ruled out because they were deemed to be too synonymous with royalty and had been home to Northern Ireland governors since partition. According to senior retired NIO civil servant Mary Madden from West Belfast, Julian King, for whom she was working, decided an alternative venue had to be found. King, who had been attached to the British Embassy in Dublin, had distinguished himself planning and cooperating with the Irish government for the Queen's visit in 2011. Madden advises me that one day, as she was driving by the Lyric Theatre in Stranmillis, it occurred to her that the Lyric would be an appropriate venue for the meeting because it would provide 'an arts environment' devoid of any political overtones. King bought into this idea. Mary Madden liaised with Mark Carruthers, who was the chairman of the Lyric Theatre, and he cleared the decks to facilitate the meeting involving Queen Elizabeth, McGuinness and Robinson.

We rarely get an insight into the background to what exactly goes on in the planning of a royal visit. These trips are planned months, if not years, ahead. There is always something in the calendar to which the Queen will have to go or to which a member of her family will have to go. Everything is hush-hush, on a need-to-know basis. This Diamond Jubilee visit was one such moment.

In the case of Northern Ireland, there was always an extraordinary sensitivity attached to royal visits. The Queen was regularly steered in the direction of Bangor, Coleraine, Newtownards and Lisburn – all solid unionist, Protestant towns or cities. Fundamentally, this was because the establishment didn't want any public display of hostility visited upon the royal family and, of course, security was always a factor. In July 1966, a piece of a block was dropped on the bonnet of the Queen's Rolls-Royce in Belfast during a visit to open the new Queen Elizabeth II Bridge. A teenager working on the Chamber of Commerce building was arrested and charged. That was history. The world was changing and so, too, were the dynamics for this royal visit.

The 'think tank' inside Sinn Féin decided that it would be helpful and potentially useful to remove some of the 'edge' which might remain within sections of the republican family arising from any handshake between the Queen and McGuinness. Pressure quickly grew for the inclusion of Irish President Michael D. Higgins and his wife, Sabina, in the Lyric events of the day. Sinn Féin saw this as 'equivalence', in a sense involving the two heads of State in the encounter. King and Geidt had no objections to this. At this point, Co-operation Ireland, of which Peter Sheridan was chief executive, became involved in further underscoring the north–south dimension of the Queen's visit.

On Wednesday morning, 27 June 2012, Martin McGuinness, his special advisor Vincent Parker, their driver and another associate, on their way to the Lyric Theatre, went for breakfast in Maggie Mays Belfast Café, on the Malone Road opposite Methodist College. Students lined up to get their photographs taken with the deputy first minister and to shake hands with him. Little did they know that the hand they shook that morning would be shaking hands with the Queen that very day. McGuinness had no extra security travelling to the Lyric that morning. The planned meeting and handshakes between the Queen and the first and deputy first ministers were choreographed well in advance, to take place in the McGrath Suite on the ground floor of the theatre overlooking the River Lagan, well away from the public gaze and a posse of press. Regrettably the beautiful view over the Lagan was blacked out. The windows had been fitted with heavy-duty curtains to make sure that no snooping camera folk could film from the other side of the river using a long lens. Despite all those involved in the detailed security of the planned encounter, I am advised that it was NIO official Ken Mack who alerted security chiefs to the risk that might arise from uncurtained windows.

The VIPs, actors and other individuals from the arts community had assembled upstairs in the Lyric's large auditorium well ahead of the arrival of the royal party. Among the special guests who were there to meet the Queen was artist Colin Davidson, who is very well known for his portraits of actors, writers, politicians and latterly portraits of the Queen and Michael D. Higgins. The Queen was said to be a lady given to punctuality. When she arrived at the theatre, having been driven from Hillsborough Castle, she made it known to some of those looking after her that she was not happy about being ten minutes late. She took people within earshot by surprise, making an issue of this. There was even greater surprise when Prince Philip interrupted and said to her, 'It was you. You are 10 minutes late, speaking to your bloody staff.' There were times when you had to admire the 'aul boy'.

On arrival at the Lyric, the Queen was directed with Prince Philip into the McGrath Suite where her principal guests were already waiting for her. Those who were there included a cameraman with a purely royal household brief, and Christopher Geidt. Geidt introduced the Queen to Peter Robinson and Martin McGuinness, according to an eyewitness. Commenting on the private handshake between the Queen and the Sinn Féin deputy first minister, my source said, 'Martin McGuinness, like the Queen herself, displayed a certain nervousness. Once the handshakes had taken place, they all sat down and the tension seemed to disappear. The Queen didn't wear gloves for the handshakes. They had a cup of coffee and the conversation lasted 10 to 15 minutes.' The royal household cameraman captured the first handshake between the Queen and Martin McGuinness. That shot has not seen the light of day. Artist Colin Davidson gave the Queen a tour of his many portraits hanging in the Lyric of distinguished actors, including Liam Neeson. The entire visit ended with the Queen bidding McGuinness and Robinson farewell just inside the door, before being whisked away.

The local photographer chosen to capture some of the standout moments during the Queen's visit to the Lyric Theatre was Paul Faith of the Press Association. Paul has covered practically everything over the last thirty years in Northern

Ireland. He told me, 'We knew something was coming up, that Martin McGuinness was going to meet the Queen. There had been speculation among journalists that there was going to be a handshake involving the Queen and McGuinness. I was told about the meeting about a week and a half prior to the visit. I was told I would be the one photographer, apart from the royal household's own cameraman, who would be involved. The night before the visit I was officially instructed by my boss Deric Henderson that I was literally to take the photograph and not report or tell anybody about anything I had overheard.'

Faith added, 'On the morning of the meeting, the media had established that it was taking place at the Lyric Theatre. Hordes of journalists and photographers were all kept down by the bank of the River Lagan. I was in the Lyric a good two and a half hours before the Queen arrived. One of the Close Protection Unit guys said to me: "You are the only one taking a photograph of the meeting. I would not like to be you. If you mess up this, you won't be back again."'

Faith continued, 'The public handshake had to take place with the departure. Myself and the royal TV cameraman were held upstairs with the other invited guests, as the Queen and the duke, Robinson and McGuinness met in the McGrath Suite. They then came up to the main auditorium. McGuinness seemed to be holding back at the beginning. I rolled up my eyes and implied he should come forward. Peter Robinson was already at the front, closer to the Queen. McGuinness acted accordingly. I was making as much hay as possible when the sun shone, to get as many images of McGuinness and the Queen together. McGuinness seemed very relaxed. Up until about 10 minutes before the handshake took place, I still wasn't sure if it was happening. They disappeared from that area of the auditorium and we were told to go downstairs and wait for the departure. We were told the Queen would emerge from the left. She shook hands with Martin McGuinness and Robinson and that was it. It was a good, firm handshake and both of them were very relaxed and the handshake seemed to have gone on for a good while. McGuinness said his handshake was longer than Robinson's. It was obviously an historic handshake and they clearly wanted to give us as much time as possible to capture this image for history. The whole thing was over then and the Queen and the duke left.'

The Head of VIP in the Police Service of Northern Ireland during the Queen's 2012 visit to Northern Ireland was Superintendent Gerry Murray, an Ardoyne Catholic like former President Mary McAleese. Murray was by the Queen's side everywhere she went. Her security was his responsibility. In a discreet moment, Queen Elizabeth presented Murray with a set of cufflinks stamped with the letters E.R. (standing for 'Elizabeth Regina'). The Queen told him, 'The next time I am over Gerry I want to see you wearing them.'

There was no next time. The Queen died in 2022.

There was a sequel to the Lyric Theatre royal event. Paul Faith said, 'I went the next day to cover the Irish Open at Portrush and I came into the press room and Martin McGuinness spotted me and all the national photographers were there and he called out, "There's Paul" and he said to me, "You have made me famous again", and he asked one of his officials to take a photograph of "myself with him".' I doubt if any photograph Faith has taken, has ever travelled so far and so frequently as that handshake between the Queen and the late Martin McGuinness.

Epilogue

ON WRITING THE FINAL lines of this account of my forty-eight years as a journalist/broadcaster – many of which involved covering bombings, shootings and killings in these islands – I rejoice in the fact that today's children are not growing up in such a poisonous atmosphere.

I celebrate another fact: that I survived to share my life with my wife, Detta, and the children. Unlike many homes, Catholic and Protestant, across the land, we are so blessed now as grandparents to have our children's families sitting at our dinner table.

I am pleased also to be the bearer of good news in my advancing years. I can confidently state, informed by research and experience on the ground as a journalist in Northern Ireland, that 'the bad old days' are not coming back. My contention that the IRA's militant campaign belongs to yesterday is underpinned by the upward swing in electoral support for Sinn Féin on the island of Ireland, North and South. That party continues to make serious inroads electorally into the traditional heartlands of politics in the Republic of Ireland, which until recently were dominated decade after decade either by Fine Gael or Fianna Fáil. In the 2022 Assembly election in Northern Ireland and in the 2023 local government council elections, Sinn Féin emerged in both cases as the largest party. Uniquely on this island, Sinn Féin has women at the helm: Mary Lou McDonald as president and Michelle O'Neill as vice-president. The Sinn Féin hierarchy has cleverly tapped into one big reality. Women are no longer subservient to males. They are competing, matching and emulating them at all levels in society. Sinn Féin's new women councillors are uncontaminated by violence. They are part of a gym-going, politically aware, sophisticated, well-educated generation with whom first-time voters connect easily.

This new brand of Sinn Féin public representative is a game-changer on this island. Constitutional republicanism is on a solid footing, increasingly appealing to young people. This, however, is not the whole story contributing to sweeping electoral change in the nationalist community. Yesterday's hubristic credo that 'armed struggle' was the only way to realise political change is an anachronism today. The traditional anti-violence, middle-class nationalist, who voted for the SDLP and who could not countenance voting for Sinn Féin as long as violence remained, has shifted too – as witnessed in the recent council elections. The yoke of guilt due to violence has been removed. This means Sinn Féin as an electoral option is increasingly treated like any other normal constitutional party. On the other hand, unionism – a victim of ongoing splits and divisions – is a waning force in an economically weakened Northern Ireland in the wake of Brexit. Statistics point to an ageing unionist population, with nationalists enjoying a younger age profile.

My narrative that the IRA violence of over thirty years is dead and buried has to be tempered with one caveat: all my working life, the unionist war cry has been 'Ulster will fight and Ulster will be right'. Were there to be a border poll or an attempt to change the status of Northern Ireland, would loyalists become the new IRA, and if they did, against whom would they fight? England? The Republic of Ireland? Hopefully this will not come to pass. It's my dream that the children of tomorrow won't ever have to live through what my generation experienced and what children in Ukraine, Gaza and Israel have been enduring.

I know myself to be a complex individual (deemed by others to be eccentric) in whom, for decades, a jangle of warring thoughts and emotions have resided. I have always lusted for knowledge, new words and insights into individuals. I was instinctively, insatiably inquisitorial from a young age. Inevitably, factors like geography, birthplace, parents, education, religion and philosophy all played their part in shaping me. Was it vanity, arrogance or insecurity which attracted me to a performing way of life, in broadcasting? I revelled at being in the faces of people in public life with my camera or microphone, loosing off a volley of questions. There was something instinctive in me about holding people to account. Was this down to my memories of hard times growing up in isolation on the side of a hill in South Armagh? Perhaps it was. With the ceasefires in place in the nineties, journalism changed and I changed too. In a way, I reinvented myself, becoming more involved in social media and documentary filmmaking – culminating in hosting my own TV series annually on UTV called *Eamonn Mallie: Face to Face with* ... These have been extended interviews with high-profile people like former Prime Minister Tony Blair, Eamonn Holmes, Patrick Kielty, Adrian Dunbar, Andrea Corr and dozens more. These interviews are the antithesis of those I used to do when holding people in power to account. In this case, the tone of the interviews is more conversational, allowing guests to be more expansive about the sweep of their lives.

In my professional life, I was rarely left speechless. I lived one of those moments while interviewing RTÉ's *Late Late Show* host Patrick Kielty, whose 45-year-old father was shot dead by loyalists in his Dundrum office in County Down on 25 January 1988. Sixteen-year-old Kielty was in school when he was called to the headteacher's office to be informed about his father's killing. In his narrative about that day, Patrick revealed to me that it was only when he heard me reading the details of the shooting dead of his father later that evening on Downtown Radio that it sank in that he was actually dead. He told me, 'I will always remember your reporting those details about my father.' I felt so helpless at that moment.

During the Troubles, my escape hatch from that dark world was Detta's broad smile greeting me, along with the excitement of the children on seeing me, when I walked through the door. Literature, art collecting and poetry reading were also useful outlets in a bleak world. In more recent years, I published my first collection of poetry, titled *Under the Tilley Lamp*. Hopefully, as I scale back more poems will find me!

I continue to be prayerful. My salvation is uppermost in my mind. I seek out beauty in everything I do, despite all my own failings and the ever-present ugliness and brutal war images on our screens nightly from Ukraine and Gaza. Words still excite me – none more than this invocation in Latin: *Agnus Dei, qui tollis peccata mundi, miserere nobis. Agnus Dei, qui tollis peccata mundi, miserere nobis. Agnus Dei, qui tollis peccata mundi, dona nobis pacem.*

I love the musicality of those words.

One of my all-time-favourite singer-songwriters is Kris Kristofferson, whom Detta and I saw in Belfast in the King's Hall many years ago. These words which he penned will be fine on my headstone:

Why me Lord, what have I ever done
To deserve even one
Of the pleasures I've known?